MY OLD
Kentucky
ROAD TRIP
★

THE STATE OF BOURBON

EXPLORING THE SPIRIT OF KENTUCKY

CAMERON M. LUDWICK

&

BLAIR THOMAS HESS

Photography by ELLIOTT HESS

INDIANA UNIVERSITY PRESS

This book is a publication of

Indiana University Press
Office of Scholarly Publishing
Herman B Wells Library 350
1320 East 10th Street
Bloomington, Indiana 47405 USA

iupress.indiana.edu

The paper used in this publication meets the minimum
requirements of the American National Standard
for Information Sciences—Permanence of Paper for
Printed Library Materials, ANSI Z39.48-1992.

Manufactured in the United States of America

Cataloging information is available from the Library of Congress.

ISBN 978-0-253-03781-7 (paperback)
ISNB 978-0-253-03466-3 (ebook)

1 2 3 4 5   23 22 21 20 19 18

All photos by Elliott Hess unless otherwise noted,
www.elliotthess.com.

To our fellow proud and thirsty Kentuckians. May the barrels in our rackhouses always outnumber us, may bourbon always flow through the hearts of us, and may we always have a fellow Kentuckian to share a glass with us. Cheers.

Contents

Acknowledgments

We like to tell folks that we aren't writers who travel, we're travelers who happen to write. Such is the case that none of the *My Old Kentucky Road Trip* (*MOKRT*) books would be possible without a great deal of help along our journeys.

We are so thankful to all of our fellow Kentuckians we meet on our trips. Whether they are out exploring their great state like we are, working at one of Kentucky's amazing state parks where we stay on all of our overnight trips, or leading tours at the distilleries we've spent days and days traversing, we appreciate what each contributes to our travels.

Facing: Elliott Louise Hess, age one, high-fives longtime Wild Turkey Master Distiller and Kentucky bourbon legend Jimmy Russell at the brand's distillery in Lawrenceburg.

We also owe a great debt to the Master Distillers across the state who help keep the history and tradition of bourbon alive while maintaining a visionary course to ensure its future. Consider giving your visitor center staffs a raise—we've seen them herd some major crowds on busy weekends at your distilleries without even batting an eye or losing their smiles. It's not only impressively professional, it's so very Kentuckian.

Of course, we are grateful for our family and friends who supported our first *MOKRT* project and who gave us the courage and sanity to embark on yet another adventure.

Thanks to the incomparable Ashley Runyon at Indiana University Press, who not only gave us this opportunity but who provided advice and friendship along the way. We can't express how appreciative we are of that.

And since we're already out of words, it is impossible to articulate our gratitude to Alice Speilburg at Speilburg Literary Agency. While we did the fun stuff, you helped us navigate the tough parts of this journey with an unyielding calm. And you even managed to keep us on schedule! We are forever thankful for your professional guidance and for your years of friendship.

Thanks to our amazingly talented photographer, Elliott Hess (**www.elliotthess.com**), for his hard work, dedication, hours of travel, and comic relief on these road trips. This book wouldn't be the same without your images.

And finally, to our newest and littlest roadtripper: you crawled the rock floors of Mammoth Cave before you could walk, you visited your first Civil War battle reenactment before you could talk, and we've been chasing you across Kentucky ever since. You've made our lives better and our road trips more entertaining, Elliott Louise. Thanks for teaching us that bourbon barrel warehouses echo.

— *Blair and Cameron*

THE STATE
OF BOURBON

Introduction

As any traveling Kentuckian can attest, there are a few predictable things that the state is universally known for. "You're from Kentucky?" they'll always ask. "So you must know a lot about . . ." All born-and-bred—or adopted—Bluegrass citizens know where this is going, right?

Horses. Fried chicken. Bourbon.

Never mind that Kentucky has more claims to fame than one can count (think the tommy gun, traffic lights, the "Happy Birthday" song, cheeseburgers, steamboats, the high five, couch burning, and the Clooneys), it's all about the infamous trifecta.

Once, while on vacation across the pond in Newcastle, England, we found a pub that boasted a "Kentucky Cola" that was made with Coca-Cola and Jack Daniels. Someone neglected to do his or her research on that one. These proud Kentuckians were downright offended by that Tennessee whiskey being poured into our Kentucky bourbon cocktail, and you can be sure we were quick to correct them. Y'all can hardly expect ladies to stand for such a travesty.

Bourbon is trendy these days, and around the globe, interest in bourbon is growing rapidly. But as Kentuckians, this is nothing new. Welcome to the state where bourbon barrels outnumber residents—and no, we're not joking. While distilleries welcome more visitors than ever and the most exclusive, rare bourbons are getting harder and harder to track down, most Kentuckians have

Facing: Woodford Reserve Distillery in Versailles.

a whole cupboard full at home. And we'll drink it neat, thank you very much.

The rest of the world is just catching up, and they are thirsty for and fascinated by anything related to this unique corn whiskey, so as Kentuckians, we are the unofficial ambassadors of our famed libation. In that English pub a few years ago as we attempted to educate the bartender on the difference between Tennessee whiskey and Kentucky bourbon, it wasn't surprising that he concluded, "Oh, so one is made in Tennessee and the other where you're from?" We politely let the "where you're from" generalization pass without brandishing our state flag key chains and climbing up on a bar stool to sing "My Old Kentucky Home."

It's the uninitiated's usual reply: Bourbon comes from Kentucky! While "Kentucky Straight" bourbon must come from the Bluegrass State, the law puts no such restriction on all bourbons. But here's the thing—bourbon *is* Kentucky. Its craftsmanship and flavors cannot be separated from the culture and history of our land, nor will they ever be. It's a bold claim, sure, but despite the (modest) rise of non-Kentucky-based distilleries around the world, the most recognizable brands, the favorite batches, and the overwhelming market share belong to Kentucky bourbon.

The history and heritage of our native spirit lives on in the stills and rackhouses of the stops along the Kentucky Bourbon Trail, its craft tours, and the Urban Bourbon Trail. But this is not a guide to these trails. Neither is it a tasting guide nor a cocktail book (though we'll be sure to throw in some of our favorites). It's a road trip through bourbon's beginnings. It's an adventure that stretches from east to west just like the earliest settlers of Kentucky laid our foundation. It's a journey to try to explain why bourbon runs through our veins.

On a hot summer day at the Wild Turkey Distillery in Lawrenceburg, an older man sat in the corner of the visitor's center making small talk with folks who had traveled from all over to see how bourbon is made. To most, he looked like one of them—a tourist there for a history lesson and a free sample.

But to the trained eye, this was Jimmy Russell, longtime Master Distiller at Wild Turkey and a bourbon legend in his own right.

"You come for the bourbon, but you stay for the stories. Bourbon tells the best stories," he told us. So in that spirit, join us as we journey across Kentucky to the lesser-known landmarks of bourbon history. We think you'll find it really does have quite a few great stories to tell.

While on this My Old Kentucky Road Trip, *as you should on all road trips, we ask that you designate a sober driver.*

"Keep your friends close and your bourbon closer."

—*Old Kentucky proverb*
(Trust us, it's true.)

Part One
BOURBON FIRSTS

To start out on this road trip, one could consider the age-old question: which came first, the chicken or the egg? Before you spend the first fifty parkway miles arguing that one, let us rephrase. Which came first, Kentucky or bourbon? And if you can answer that, riddle us this: Who made it first? Where was it first made? Who first sold it?

Making your case for who should get the front seat on this road trip may be easier than winning one of the arguments above. You see, Kentuckians have been drinking bourbon and arguing about its origins for centuries. Yes, centuries. Generations of Kentuckians have distilled bourbon, and while many hold claims to fame as the first or the best, it is difficult to accurately identify who first made it and where bourbon officially got its start.

Here's what we can agree on: Kentuckians have been distilling bourbon whiskey, which is at least 51 percent corn combined with other grains and aged in new charred oak barrels, and enjoying the fruits of their labor for longer than anyone can remember. The distinctive smell of its sour mash has wafted through the rolling hills of central Kentucky since the first pioneers followed buffalo trails through the Appalachian Mountains.

Bourbon was born here, so let's start with its roots. We'll travel across central Kentucky from Louisville to Frankfort and Lawrenceburg to Cox's Creek and Loretto to Lexington and discover where bourbon was realized.

1 | The First Kentucky Bourbon

The origins of "Kentucky Straight Bourbon Whiskey" date back to days before state boundaries were drawn, when early governances encouraged corn cultivation. Pioneers discovered that corn was not only easy to grow, but it also made a very distinctive and somewhat lighter style of whiskey.

Trying to name the first person to make whiskey is like arguing with your grandmother over the exact recipe of her famous chocolate pie. No one really knows the answer. There are reports that General James Wilkinson built a distillery at Harrodsburg in 1774, Kentucky's earliest permanent settlement, but conflicting articles don't put Wilkinson in the state until a decade later.

Others say it was Daniel Boone's second, third, eighth, or something cousin Wattie, and then some say bourbon got its start in Nelson County. There are other names out there, too, like Joseph and Samuel Davis, James Garrard, and William Calk. Anyone from Kentucky will tell you that more than half of its multigenerational families can trace their lineage back far enough to a long-lost, great-great-great-somebody who most certainly probably also invented the state's famed libation. Maybe they all did make bourbon whiskey. Maybe their product just wasn't good enough to become a long-lasting brand.

One name that appears over and over in bourbon's early history is that of Virginia preacher Elijah Craig.

Elijah Craig is a man of great notoriety for his role in the settlement of the area of Virginia that would become Kentucky, so it is only natural that he is credited by some to be the inventor of bourbon. He was a Baptist preacher, born in 1738 in Orange County, Virginia, which is notably home to President James Madison's Montpelier. At the time, Baptists were considered a fairly controversial denomination, and while they were protected by Virginia's freedom of religion laws, Baptists faced enough challenges that Craig became very involved in politics and dedicated to protecting religious freedom federally.

Craig's brother, Lewis, led an exodus of more than six hundred people west in 1781 in search of more religious freedom. Elijah followed his brother a year later and purchased one thousand acres in what was then Fayette County, Virginia, where he established a town called Lebanon in 1784. But this is not the Lebanon located in Marion County that many Kentuckians know today. This Lebanon was renamed to its current moniker, Georgetown, in 1790 in honor of President George Washington.

There, Elijah Craig founded several churches and the first classical school in Kentucky in 1787. And he didn't stop there. He went on to become an entrepreneur and successful businessman,

Georgetown is home to some of the earliest days of Kentucky bourbon.

building the first paper mill and fulling mill—for the manufacturing of cloth—in the state. And in 1789, he started a distillery in what is now part of present-day Woodford and Scott counties.

You'll find some old news stories that say that it was in this distillery that he invented bourbon—a version of whiskey that requires a mashbill of at least 51 percent corn, aged in new charred oak barrels, entered into the barrel for aging at no more than 125 proof, and bottled at 80 proof or more. We've heard more than one account along the Bourbon Trail that Craig was the first to age his whiskey in charred oak barrels, which gives bourbon its distinctive honey-brown coloring. But ask around, and you'll find that not everyone is convinced.

Elijah Craig died in Georgetown in 1808 and is buried at Stamping Ground Baptist Church, which was originally founded as McConnell's Church by Craig.

Regardless of the official pioneering genius behind the corn whiskey, Kentuckians still toast Mr. Craig—and his namesake bourbon produced by Heaven Hill Distillery in Bardstown—for his contributions to the state and to the bourbon industry.

★ A ROAD TRIP TO GEORGETOWN ★

Elijah Craig founded Georgetown. Located ten miles north of Lexington off I-75, Georgetown is thought by many to be where Kentucky bourbon whiskey was first produced. Royal Spring, still visible today at Royal Spring Park on West Main Street, provided the water for Elijah Craig to make his bourbon. Today, Royal Spring is the state's largest spring-based public water system, serving more than seven thousand customers.

Georgetown College is also located downtown. Elijah Craig founded the college in 1787. It is the oldest Baptist college west of the Allegheny Mountains.

★ IF YOU GO ▸ Georgetown

Make sure to check out other area attractions while you're near downtown. Visit the authentic 1874 log cabin built by former slave Milton Leach, also located at Royal Spring Park downtown. Then take a walking tour of downtown's historic architecture. Georgetown has more than two hundred buildings listed on the National Register of Historic Places. Head to historic

Royal Spring located in Georgetown is thought by many to be the source of water from which the first Kentucky bourbon whiskey was produced. Still visible at Royal Spring Park on West Main Street, it is now the state's largest spring-based public water system.

Elijah Craig Kentucky Straight Bourbon Whiskey is distilled by Heaven Hill. Elijah Craig is often credited as the father of bourbon, but many dispute that he was the first to distill the famous spirit.

Ward Hall, on US 460 just a mile outside of downtown. Completed in 1853, Ward Hall is one of the largest Greek Revival structures in Kentucky. Other points of interest include the Cardome Renaissance Centre, Toyota Motor Manufacturing (you can take a tour and see cars built!), and Evans Orchard and Cider Mill, a great agritourism destination with you-pick apples, fresh cider, and pumpkins in the fall.

A ROAD TRIP TO
★ HEAVEN HILL DISTILLERY ★

Heaven Hill Distillery was founded in Louisville in 1935 by a group of investors that included the Shapira family and prominent distiller Joseph L. Beam, first cousin to the well-known Jim Beam. Joe Beam was the brand's first Master Distiller, along with his youngest son, Harry. Descendants of the Shapira family still own and run the company today, and all of the brand's Master Distillers have been members of the Beam family.

It was started as Old Heavenhill Springs Distillery and has predominately focused on its two flagship labels, Evan Williams and Elijah Craig. But today, Heaven Hill produces a variety of bourbons, including Bernheim Original, Pikesville Straight Rye, Rittenhouse Rye, Henry McKenna Single Barrel, Parker's Heritage Collection, and Larceny Kentucky Straight Bourbon, as well as various other malts and vodkas.

Today, Heaven Hill's bottling facility, many of its warehouses, and the Bourbon Heritage Center are located in Bardstown.

★ IF YOU GO   **Heaven Hill Distillery**

While some of the operations remain in Louisville, you'll get the best road trip experience if you visit Heaven Hill's Bourbon Heritage Center and tasting room in Bardstown. Check out **heavenhilldistillery.com** for prices and hours of operation, which vary based on the time of year.

A ROAD TRIP TO THE
★ BIRTHPLACE OF BOURBON ★

In central Kentucky, just northeast of Lexington, roadtrippers may stumble on Bourbon County. While travelers often assume that Bourbon County must be the home of bourbon (what's in a name, and all that), it isn't the case at all. In fact, Bourbon County, Kentucky, which was established as part of Virginia in 1785 and later transferred to the Commonwealth of Kentucky in 1792, was actually named in honor of the French royal House of Bourbon. The House of Bourbon was a branch of the Capetian dynasty, who first ruled France and Navarre in the sixteenth century. While bourbon was made in and shipped from Bourbon County—quite a lot of it actually, there were many distilleries in this area that encompassed about twenty-seven present-day counties—bourbon actually got its name from the county and not the other way around. Bourbon County was one of the first counties established in Kentucky (it was founded before Kentucky was even a state), and as barrels of corn whiskey were loaded on steamboats for shipping, the barrels were stamped with "BOURBON," indicating the place from which they were being sent. Merchants began referring to the barrels as "barrels of Bourbon," leading to the adoption of the name. It gives you a whole different perspective on the importance of luggage tags, doesn't it?

But to find the true birthplace of bourbon, you need to travel a bit west of Paris to the valleys along the Kentucky River where the current meanders northwest and cuts through present-day Woodford, Scott, and Franklin counties. Interstate 64 crosses the Kentucky River just south of Frankfort. Below the bridge, the river curves south around a bend where it meets the bank of Glenn's Creek just out of sight from the cars zipping down the highway.

If you travel KY 1659—locally known as Glenn's Creek Road, which turns into McCracken Pike—as it stretches between Frankfort and Versailles, you will pass through some of the original foundations of bourbon.

An empty bourbon rackhouse sits along KY 1659, a road that follows the Kentucky River and Glenn's Creek, both of which were great sources of limestone-rich water for Kentucky's earliest distilleries.

Along the wide banks of the Kentucky River sit some of the state's original bourbon barrel houses. As you pass, take a closer look, and you'll find some of the brick walls turning black. It isn't soot; it's *Baudoinia compniacensis*, a species of black mold sometimes called "whiskey fungus" that feeds on the ethanol vapor released by liquor as it ages. As you visit distilleries across the Bluegrass State, you'll find this black discoloration at all of them. Be cautiously curious. The mold isn't bad to touch or breathe in moderation. In fact, many houses in neighborhoods around Louisville's large distilling district, Shively, battle the whiskey fungus, too. But mold is still mold, so you don't want to ingest it or breathe it in directly.

Just west of the iconic barrel houses on Glenn's Creek Road and south of Frankfort near the Millville town limits sits the Old Taylor Distillery. This eighty-two-acre plot of land is rich in the history of bourbon and the culture of its earliest crafters and drinkers.

Edmond Haynes Taylor is a true bourbon baron. After his father died, he spent time living with his uncle Zachary Taylor (as in President Zachary Taylor) before moving in with his other

The historic and picturesque Old Taylor Distillery in Franklin County. Originally built in the late 1800s by Colonel E. H. Taylor Jr., today it is being revitalized as Castle and Key Distillery with Kentucky's first female Master Distiller, Marianne Barnes, at its helm.

uncle, E. H. Taylor, and adding the suffix *junior* to his name out of respect. He worked in bourbon for a large part of his life, starting out at Gaines, Berry, & Co., home to Old Crow Bourbon, and then going on to buy and expand the Old Fashioned Copper Distillery in Frankfort, which is known today as Buffalo Trace. After parting ways with his business partners, Colonel E. H. Taylor Jr. opened Old Taylor Distillery in 1887.

In addition to his role as a leader in the whiskey industry, Colonel Taylor served as the mayor of Frankfort for sixteen years and then as a state representative and senator. His political influence helped him revitalize the bourbon industry, which was suffering from a lack of consumer confidence due to product quality. Taylor worked to pass laws to ensure a higher standard, including the Bottled-in-Bond Act of 1897, which provided a federal tax subsidy for distilleries who followed certain standards. Colonel Taylor knew good bourbon, and he wanted to ensure that each consumer got a good bottle of bourbon every time. Old Taylor Distillery was the first to produce one million US government–certified cases of straight bourbon whiskey.

His distillery was a showcase of bourbon making in Kentucky. The picturesque property featured a peristyle springhouse, stone bridges, gazebos, sunken gardens, and castle-like buildings complete with turrets, all built from Kentucky limestone. After the distillery closed in 1972, Mother Nature tried her hardest to reclaim these beautifully crafted structures. But in 2016, Kentucky's first female Master Distiller, Marianne Barnes, managed to revitalize the property, tradition, and the bourbon that ran through its veins, establishing Castle and Key Distillery—the castle part in honor of the limestone buildings' castle-like appearance, and the key for the key-shaped pool filled with fresh limestone water hiding under the springhouse.

★ IF YOU GO   **Castle and Key Distillery**

As of this book's publication, Castle and Key's bourbons and ryes are still aging, but the distillery will also be selling Gin and Vodka. You can book a behind-the-scenes tour of their restoration and distilling efforts through their website: **castleandkey.com** and follow their progress on social media.

Other Early Bourbon Pioneers

It took more than just one man (or woman) to bring whiskey making to where it is today. Here are some other pioneering families who helped invent Kentucky bourbon:

Elijah Pepper (James E. Pepper and Old Crow bourbons) settled in Old Pepper Springs, Kentucky, in 1776.

Robert Samuels (Maker's Mark bourbon) settled in Kentucky in 1780.

Jacob Beam (Jim Beam bourbon) arrived in Kentucky in 1785. Jim Beam sold his first barrel of whiskey in 1795.

The Brown family (Old Forester bourbon) came to Kentucky in 1792.

Daniel Weller (W. L. Weller bourbon) arrived in Kentucky in 1794.

2 | **The State's First Bourbon Distillery**

A ROAD TRIP TO THE
★ EVAN WILLIAMS BOURBON ★
EXPERIENCE

It is difficult to believe that anyone with the knowledge and equipment required to make whiskey would only produce enough for himself. So, it is very possible that the early settlers of the state were selling and bartering with whiskey long before the first official distillery opened its doors for production. But Evan Williams actually did build a real distillery in Louisville in 1783, which is believed by most—while doubted by some historians—to be the first commercial distillery on record.

It is probable that no one will ever really know the identity of Kentucky's first distiller. In the state's early days, there was no tax on distilled spirits, which means there are no official government records on any distillers. Illiteracy could also contribute to the lack of records.

But even if Mr. Williams wasn't the first, he was among the earliest operators of many commercial distilleries that would pop up across Kentucky.

Williams was an entrepreneur and politician who emigrated from Wales in the 1780s. He was a farmer, building contractor, harbormaster, businessman, inventor, and civic leader who built a distillery on the banks of the Ohio River. Today, the distillery no longer stands, but Evan Williams lives on in the world of bourbon.

Evan Williams brand Kentucky Straight Bourbon Whiskey is distilled at Heaven Hill Distillery in Louisville and bottled in Bardstown. The brand now includes several varieties, including a nine-year-old single barrel, flavored bourbons, and a white label version. It is consistently a leading seller of straight bourbon.

★ IF YOU GO ▸ The Evan Williams Bourbon Experience

While Evan Williams is produced in Louisville and stored and bottled in Bardstown by Heaven Hill, the Evan Williams Bourbon Experience, located at 528 Main Street, a few blocks from Louisville's historic Whiskey Row, is the place to visit to learn about and taste the brand. Visit **evanwilliams.com.**

Visitors get a unique perspective on bourbon during tours through the Evan Williams Bourbon Experience in the heart of Whiskey Row in downtown Louisville.

Facing: Visitors of all ages enjoy distillery tours at Buffalo Trace in Frankfort. Visit www.buffalotracedistillery.com for tour information.

A ROAD TRIP TO
★ BUFFALO TRACE DISTILLERY ★

We warned you before we started—the only thing we can agree on is that we don't agree where bourbon got its start. Case in point: forget all that stuff we just told you about Evan Williams; Buffalo Trace Distillery says it is the oldest continuously operating distillery in the United States (though Burks's distillery, now used for production of Maker's Mark, makes the same claim and is officially registered as such in the *Guinness Book of World Records*). It remained open during Prohibition and was allowed to bottle alcohol for medicinal purposes and even distill some during the final years of the alcohol ban.

Buffalo Trace Distillery, previously known as the George T. Stagg Distillery and the O.F.C. Distillery, is nestled on the banks of the Kentucky River in Frankfort. The distillery claims the sprawling property is located on what was once one of many ancient buffalo crossings—hence the namesake bourbon brand, Buffalo Trace Kentucky Straight Bourbon Whiskey, which was introduced in August 1999—that helped the first pioneers carve a path through Kentucky. The distillery is listed on the National

The Kentucky State Capitol building in Frankfort.

Register of Historic Places and was designated a National Historic Landmark in 2013.

Distilling began on the property in 1775 by brothers Hancock and Willis Lee. Commodore Richard Taylor constructed the first building on site in 1792 (which still stands), and Harrison Blanton built the first distillery in 1812. The distillery was purchased by Colonel Edmund H. Taylor in 1870, who named it the Old Fashioned Copper (O.F.C.) Distillery before selling it eight years later to George T. Stagg. Are these names sounding familiar? Old Taylor, Stagg, and Blanton's are some of the best bourbons around, and all are produced by Buffalo Trace.

Today, in addition to its namesake label, Buffalo Trace produces Eagle Rare, O.F.C. Vintages, Single Oak Project, Colonel E.H. Taylor Jr. Small Batch, Pappy Van Winkle, Stagg Jr., Blanton's the Original Single Barrel Bourbon Whiskey, Elmer T. Lee Single Barrel, Sazerac Rye (named for the distillery's parent company, Sazerac), W. L. Weller, Old Charter, Benchmark, Ancient Age, White Dog, an antique collection of their various brands, and more.

THE STATE OF BOURBON

Buffalo Trace Distillery

This scenic distillery is worth the drive to Frankfort to see the historic buildings where George T. Stagg installed the nation's first steam-heated storage warehouses and where more than 2.6 million gallons of bourbon are produced each year. While Buffalo Trace is not on the official Bourbon Trail, it does offer free tours to visitors. Special tours like ghost tours are also available throughout the year. Visit **www.buffalotracedistillery.com** for information.

While you're in Frankfort, check out the Capitol District, home to the state capitol building, Governor's Mansion, and famous Floral Clock. Daniel Boone is buried in Frankfort Cemetery off of Main Street, and Rebecca Ruth Candy offers tours of its historic candy factory, where the bourbon ball was invented.

Why Kentucky?

There is a lot of talk and speculation surrounding bourbon firsts: who was the first to make it, first to bottle it, first to drink it? But not a lot is said about why Kentucky is the place where bourbon is made so much and so well.

It starts in the state's geological foundation. Kentucky is known for the limestone that stretches under its rolling hills, and that pristine, limestone-filtered water is key to making the perfect bourbon. The state's arable land and ability to cultivate corn and grains are also contributing factors. All of the ingredients needed for whiskey were readily available to the earliest settlers in Kentucky and are still abundant to processors, distillers, and connoisseurs today.

Kentucky's seasons are also ideal. As bourbon ages in rackhouses, the outside environment plays a major factor in the magic that is taking place inside those barrels. The warm, humid Kentucky summers cause the bourbon to absorb into the wood of the charred oak barrels, soaking in the flavor. Then the state's cold, but not bitter, winters allow the barrels to retract and release the bourbon back into the barrel.

Glenn's Creek, which runs behind Woodford Reserve Distillery in Versailles and past Castle and Key Distillery in Franklin County, provides limestone-filtered water that is great for distilling bourbon. Many of the state's earliest distilleries were built along the banks of this water source.

Notice the warehouses at Wild Turkey, which sit high on a bluff overlooking the Kentucky River. Wild Turkey paints its rackhouses a light gray/brown color because they are exposed to so much sunlight. The light color repels some of that sunlight so that the warehouses don't get too hot in the summers. At Maker's Mark, which sits down low in a valley, the warehouses are painted black to help absorb the sunlight that is harder to catch between the hills.

A ROAD TRIP DOWN
★ THE BOURBON TRAIL ★

The Kentucky Distillers' Association launched the Kentucky Bourbon Trail in 1999 to promote the bourbon industry in Kentucky. In the beginning, seven of the region's eight distilleries were part of the tour. Today, ten distilleries are stops on the journey.

Tours at each of the destinations offer visitors from around the world a firsthand look at the art and science of crafting bourbon, educating them about the rich history and proud tradition of the Kentucky spirit. Every year, new attendance records are set as more than one million visitors register their tour passports and travel to distilleries along the trail.

Think about it: when you visit Scotland, you drink the scotch; travel to Russia and enjoy vodka; Italians have their wine; the Irish have their Guinness. In America—and perhaps most proudly in Kentucky—we drink bourbon. Ninety-five percent of bourbon is distilled, aged, and bottled in the Bluegrass State. More than an industry, bourbon is a culture, a history, and a heritage built up by generations of Kentuckians.

This is one of our favorite road trips—traveling to Maker's Mark, Jim Beam, Bulleit, Four Roses, Town Branch, Wild Turkey, Evan Williams, Heaven Hill, Angel's Envy, and Woodford Reserve to experience the bourbon-making process, learn about the recipes, view the state-of-the-art facilities, take in the beautiful landscapes, and taste the famous libation. Not every distillery is

Barrels of bourbon sit along a rail track at Woodford Reserve Distillery in Versailles. Rails across the distillery's property help move the five-hundred-pound barrels between buildings.

Rackhouses sit on bluffs above the Kentucky River at Wild Turkey Distillery in Lawrenceburg. The black staining on the building is the mold *Baudoinia*, known also as whiskey fungus, that feeds on the ethanol vapor released by liquor as it ages.

featured on the Bourbon Trail, but a great sampling of some of our favorite brands is included.

★ IF YOU GO ▸ The Kentucky Bourbon Trail

Remember the part about one million visitors traveling this trail annually? Consider that when you set out; the distilleries could be crowded. But the good news is that most are open seven days a week, so you have plenty of options. Summer is the busiest time of year, and Saturdays are peak days. We've enjoyed tours on Sunday afternoons and weekday mornings. That's when crowds are most manageable.

Some of our favorite things to watch out for include the scenic property of Maker's Mark, the incredibly unique Spanish architecture of Four Roses, the beautiful stills at Town Branch, and the barrels being rolled between rackhouses at Woodford Reserve. And the luckiest of visitors to Wild Turkey will catch longtime Master Distiller and bourbon legend Jimmy Russell signing bourbon bottles in the visitor's center on warm summer afternoons.

Before you go, visit **www.kybourbontrail.com** to pick up your passport! Collect stamps from each of your stops in this souvenir passport and redeem for prizes!

3 | The First Sour Mash Recipe

For you scientists out there, let's talk chemistry. Mash is a mixture of grain, malt, and water, and it's at the heart of any batch of whiskey. In the sour mash process, distillers use spent mash, or previously fermented mash that still contains live yeast, to start the fermentation of a new batch. The sour mash creates acid that controls the growth of bacteria, to avoid tainting the taste of whiskey, and that allows a proper pH balance for the yeast to work. It also ensures consistency between batches by creating an environment favorable to the particular yeast strain flavoring a

Above: Visitors on a tour of Maker's Mark Distillery in Loretto sample mash in the fermenting tanks. The bubbles are the result of the natural process of yeast breaking down sugars.

specific whiskey. The sour mash process is used for the production of every bourbon whiskey we've ever heard of. We imagine that it is possible to make bourbon without a sour mash, but it would be a small batch that's taste would never be accurately recreated and that's chemical balance couldn't be ensured. Hey, we could be persuaded to try anything once.

The oldest surviving sour mash recipe belongs to Catherine Carpenter, a Kentucky frontier woman and pioneering distiller who developed the recipe in 1818.

Catherine Spears Frye Carpenter was born in 1760 in Rockingham County, Virginia. She was well educated and a trained weaver. In 1776, she married John Frye and migrated with her family and other Shenandoah Valley neighbors to Kentucky. They settled in present-day Casey County, and after her husband died in the Battle of Blue Licks, Catherine married Adam Carpenter. Her second husband died in 1806, and the twice-widowed woman raised nine children on the Kentucky frontier (she birthed thirteen but lost four as young children).

She inherited a little more than 667 acres when her second husband died, and by raising cattle and distilling whiskey, she was able to acquire more land. She supported her family by selling the whiskey made from the sour mash recipe she developed.

Catherine died in 1848, and while her whiskey enterprise did not survive her, the sweet mash and sour recipes did.

Catherine Carpenter's Recipe for
Distilling Corn Meal Sweet Mash

According to the Catherine Carpenter Family Papers,
Kentucky Historical Society

To a hundred gallon tub put in a bushel and a half of hot water then a half a bushel of meal. Stir it well then one bushel of water and then a half bushel of meal and so on until you have mashed one bushel and a half of corn meal—Stir it all effectively then sprinkle a double handful of meal over the mash let it stand two hours then pour over the mash 2 gallons of warm water put in a half gallon of malt stir that well into the mash then stir in a half a bushel of Rye or wheat meal. Stir it well for 15 minutes put in another half gallon of malt. Stir it well and very frequently until you can bear your hand in the mash up to your wrist then put in three bushels of cold slop or one gallon of good yeast then fill up with cold water. If you use yeast put in the cold water first and then the yeast. If you have neither yeast or Slop put in three peck of Beer from the bottom of a tub.

Catherine Carpenter's Recipe for Distilling by a Sour Mash

According to the Catherine Carpenter Family Papers, Kentucky Historical Society

Put into the mash tub Six bushels of very hot slop then put in one Bushel of corn meal ground pretty course Stir well then sprinkle a little meal over the mash let it stand 5 days that is 3 full days betwist the Day you mash and the day you cool off—on the fifth day put in 3 gallons of warm water then put in one gallon of rye meal and one gallon of malt work it well into the malt and stir for 3 quarters of an hour then fill the tub half full of Luke warm water. Stir it well and with a fine sieve or otherwise Break all the lumps fine then let stand for three hours then fill up the tub with lukewarm water. For warm weather—five bushels of slop instead of six let it stand an hour and a half Instead of three hours and cold water instead of warm.

Today, distilleries take these sour mash recipes and the strains that keep them going very seriously—so seriously, in fact, that Wild Turkey Distillery in Lawrenceburg keeps eight yeast strains at secret locations hidden across the state with an additional batch stored in the basement of Master Distiller Jimmy Russell's house just a few miles from the distillery. This way, even if the distillery burned to the ground or was blown away by a natural disaster, they could get a new batch of bourbon started before the facilities were rebuilt. Now that's dedication.

A ROAD TRIP TO MAKER'S MARK TO DISCOVER WOMEN'S ROLE IN ★ THE RISE OF WHISKEY ★

While men secured jobs at all of the original distilleries as Master Distillers, women still played a significant role in the rise of the bourbon industry in Kentucky. In addition to Catherine Carpenter's sour mash fermentation technique that is still used by distillers today, Marjorie Samuels set the standard for liquor branding and packaging at Maker's Mark Distillery in Loretto, Kentucky.

Marge Samuels was born into bourbon. Her father's family cofounded the Mattingly & Moore Distillery in Bardstown in the mid-1800s, and she married Bill Samuels Sr., a sixth-generation Kentucky distiller whose family owned and operated the T. W. Samuels Distillery. The couple also happened to live next door to Colonel Jim and Mary Beam, another famous Kentucky bourbon duo.

In 1953, Marge's husband was working on a new kind of bourbon that used wheat in place of rye as the secondary grain to corn. She baked bread with a variety of alternative grains, and Bill ultimately selected red winter wheat. When it was time to

Bourbon barrels age inside a warehouse at Buffalo Trace Distillery in Frankfort.

A barrel of O.F.C. Bourbon ages inside a warehouse. This bourbon is produced by Buffalo Trace Distillery in Frankfort and is one of the brand's rarest and most collected whiskeys.

A line of the most high-end and sought-after bourbons, Pappy Van Winkle, sits on a shelf at its distillery, Buffalo Trace.

A Buffalo Trace employee packages Blanton's Bourbon at the distillery and bottling operation in Frankfort.

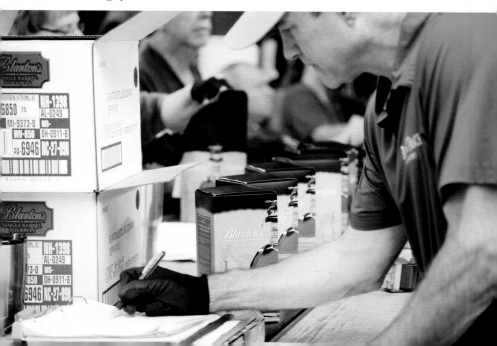

Bottles of Elmer T. Lee Single Barrel Bourbon are bottled at Buffalo Trace Distillery in Frankfort.

Bottles await their contents at Buffalo Trace Distillery in Frankfort.

A fisherman casts a line downstream from the Falls of the Ohio on the Ohio River in Louisville.

Vintage bottles of Weller and other Buffalo Trace brands sit at the distillery. Vintage collections can be viewed by visitors on tours.

Thoroughbred horses play on a late afternoon in Franklin County. The limestone-filtered water that helps make Kentucky's great bourbon is also said to grow strong-boned, fast racehorses.

Bourbon rackhouses, sometimes called warehouses or rickhouses, age barrels of the libation at Willet Distillery in Bardstown.

Old Grand-Dad 114 is a product of Jim Beam Distillery, which was founded in the late 1700s by the Beam family. Visit www .jimbeam.com for more history and for information on touring the Clermont, Kentucky, distillery.

This rackhouse, sometimes called a rickhouse or a warehouse, is at Wild Turkey Distillery in Lawrenceburg. Rackhouses store bourbon barrels while the liquor ages. This warehouse sits on top of a bluff overlooking the Kentucky River, and it is painted white in order to deflect some of Kentucky's hot summer sun so the inside temperature does not get too high. Bourbon warehouses rely only on the natural elements for heating and cooling.

These fermentation tanks are found at Maker's Mark Distillery in Loretto. The logo on the wall was developed during the distillery's beginnings by Marge Samuels, wife of Master Distiller Bill Samuels Sr.

Barrels of Maker's 46 Bourbon age in a warehouse built into the side of a hill at the distillery in Loretto.

Bottles of Maker's Mark Private Select sit on a shelf at the distillery in Loretto.

Barrels of Maker's Mark age in a warehouse at the distillery in Loretto. The colorful glass art on the ceiling is part of a temporary installation by Dale Chihuly, a favorite artist of Maker's Mark chief operation officer and eighth-generation bourbon maker, Rob Samuels.

For security reasons, bourbon barrels are locked in bonded warehouses at distilleries across the state. In this type of warehouse, the government monitors operations while the spirit ages to ensure regulations are followed.

This bonded warehouse can be found at Buffalo Trace Distillery in Frankfort.

Deer greet a stormy evening in Woodford County.

Abandoned bourbon production facilities exist in Woodford County. Some of the earliest bourbon operations were located along the Kentucky River in present-day Woodford, Scott, and Franklin counties. Many of these are being rebuilt in the midst of today's bourbon boom.

Bourbon barrels wait to be moved from filling into storage along the rails at Woodford Reserve Distillery in Woodford County. These rails are used to move the heavy barrels—which can weigh more than five hundred pounds when completely full—throughout the distillery property.

Woodford Reserve is on display for sampling in the distillery's tasting room at the visitor's center in Woodford County.

Bourbon ages in barrels in a warehouse at Woodford Reserve Distillery just outside of Versailles.

An antique pint bottle of Four Roses Whiskey was manufactured during Prohibition and sold at pharmacies for medicinal purposes. This bottle was distilled in 1914 and bottled in 1923. Four Roses was one of just six distilleries authorized to produce liquor during Prohibition.

Maker's Mark Kentucky Straight Bourbon Whisky is made at the Maker's Mark Distillery in Loretto. Maker's Mark holds the Guinness World Record as the "world's oldest operating bourbon whisky distillery . . . which has been distilling bourbon since 1805 and has been recognized as a National Historic Landmark."

The thriving Distillery District in Lexington is built on the site of the old Pepper Distillery. Today, visitors will find Ethereal Brewing, Barrel House Distilling, and a collection of bars and restaurants on this historic land. It is situated alongside Town Branch, the water supply that helped build the foundation of Lexington.

Russell's Reserve Kentucky Straight Bourbon Whiskey is made by Wild Turkey Distillery in Lawrenceburg. This bottle is autographed by longtime Master Distiller and bourbon legend Jimmy Russell. Russell and his son, Eddie, often meet tours at the visitor's center to talk about bourbon and sign bottles.

Fermenting tanks at Wild Turkey Distillery in Lawrenceburg sit under the brand's flagship labels.

Bourbon ages in barrels inside a warehouse at Wild Turkey Distillery in Lawrenceburg. Currently, there are more barrels of bourbon aging in warehouses across the state than there are people living in Kentucky.

Limestone-filtered water runs through Glenn's Creek, which flows behind Woodford Reserve and as far as Castle and Key Distillery in Woodford and Franklin counties. This creek provided water for some of the first bourbon distilleries in the state. Kentucky's abundance of limestone is credited for its fresh, clean water that is great for making bourbon.

This clock can be found at Four Roses Distillery in Lawrenceburg. The distillery offers tours at this location as well as at its bottling facility and warehouses at Cox's Creek.

Tasting glasses sit on a bourbon barrel in a rackhouse at Wild Turkey Distillery in Lawrenceburg.

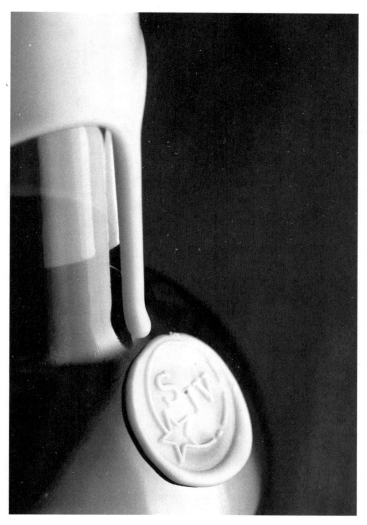

The famous red wax seals a Maker's 46 bourbon bottle. Marge Samuels, wife of the brand's first Master Distiller Bill Samuels Sr. came up with the design for the logo, which represents the fourth generation of the Samuels family (the "S" and the Roman numeral four) residing in Kentucky when the brand began.

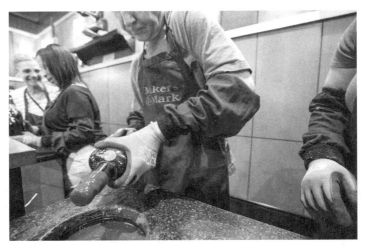

A visitor to the Maker's Mark Distillery in Loretto dips a souvenir bottle of Maker's Mark in the brand's famous red wax.

name the new brand of whiskey they had created, Marge took charge. A noted collector of fine English pewter, she knew the importance of the maker's mark in symbolizing handcrafted quality. She created the bottle and logo's lettering design printed on a hand-torn label, as well as Maker's Mark's famously unique red wax that drips down the neck of the bottle. Marge didn't have unanimous support. In fact, her husband didn't think the branding would sell and questioned his wife's design concept. But Marge Samuels had a trump card: She graduated first in their class at the University of Louisville, where the couple met. Bill finished last.

That was the end of the dinner table conversation that night and the beginning of a new era in bourbon.

Thousands of visitors—including these My Old Kentucky Road Trippers—travel to Maker's Mark Distillery in Loretto each year and line up to dip their own bottles into the famed red wax, all thanks to Marge.

In Marion County, roadtrippers may hear the tales of Mary Jane Blair, who, from 1907 to 1919, operated a distillery in an industry almost entirely dominated by men. Is anyone else having a

You-Go-Girl! moment? The Blair Distillery, known for producing Smith & Smith whiskey, which was distributed in the mid-1800s, was situated in Chicago (not the Illinois metropolis), known today as St. Francis, located about twelve miles west of Lebanon, Kentucky. Mary Jane's husband, Thomas Blair, became involved in running the distillery in 1879, and in its early days, it is said to have produced about one hundred to two hundred barrels a year. After Thomas died in 1907, Mary Jane inherited his shares of the distillery and bought out his partners before renaming the operation after herself (a move that we really, really like). Her son Nicholas helped her manage the distillery, which grew into a nine-thousand-barrel-a-year operation producing Blair's Old Club whiskey and Old Saxon. Mary Jane continued to run the operation until 1919, when the onset of Prohibition began. She died before it was repealed.

We can hardly count our affinity for drinking bourbon as impact, but women continue to make a difference in the industry today. Marianne Barnes, a Brown-Forman prodigy, was named master taster for Woodford Reserve when she was just twenty-seven. Today, she serves as the first female Master Distiller

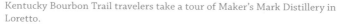
Kentucky Bourbon Trail travelers take a tour of Maker's Mark Distillery in Loretto.

since Prohibition at Castle and Key Distillery, restored from the historic Old Taylor Distillery between Frankfort and Versailles. In an industry that has been dominated by males producing a product marketed primarily to males, Marianne doesn't fit the mold—which is our absolute favorite part about her. Castle and Key released gin in 2016 made with Kentucky-grown botanicals like juniper. It is expected to release its first wheat, rye, and malt whiskeys in 2020.

★ IF YOU GO ▶ Maker's Mark Distillery

Hour-long tours are offered daily on a first-come, first-served basis at the distillery in Loretto. Wear comfortable shoes, and let the tour guides know ahead of time if you require special accommodations. Large groups are encouraged to visit on weekdays or Sundays. To learn more and to inquire about pricing, visit **tours .makersmark.com**.

Make sure you have a map, a GPS, and a smartphone—being prepared never hurts! Loretto is not far from Bardstown but can be tricky to find, depending on which direction you're coming from. We speak from experience, so trust us on this one. Helpful directions are available at **makersmark.com**.

Breaking Down the Different Mash Bills of Bourbon

The main distinction between traditional whiskey and bourbon is the grain content. Specifically, corn gives bourbon its signature flavor (and conveniently provides the highest yield of alcohol per bushel of all grains). While the corn flavor is prevalent in the liquor that comes right out of the still in the form of "White Dog"—a very generous tour guide at Town Branch once let us sample true White Dog and *phew!*—corn becomes neutral over years of aging and really lends mostly in the sweetness of the finished product.

Four Roses Distillery illustrates its mash bill of grains that go into its bourbon recipe. A bourbon must contain at least 51 percent corn.

So where do the other grains come in? Distillers have bourbon down to a science, and it's an art form for them. Every itty-bitty flavor strand is planned for and detected by their highly trained palates. But even the common connoisseurs like us can learn to pick up subtle differences.

Barley provides some malty and chocolatey flavor notes, but more important, barley lends valuable enzymes that help convert starches to sugar in the fermentation process. Bourbon is science, y'all! Rye and wheat are the main flavoring grains. Rye brings out a range of spice notes such as pepper, nutmeg, clove, and cinnamon, all of which intensify during the aging process. Rye gives bourbon the bite that it is known for. Think about that the next time you enjoy a sandwich on rye bread.

Wheat gives you a sweeter-tasting bourbon because it is not as rich as rye, thus allowing more of the sweetness of the corn and the vanilla from the charred oak barrels it is aged in to come through.

Every distillery does it a bit different—that's why touring all of them is so necessary and so much fun—but a traditional bourbon recipe is usually 70–80 percent corn with a balance of some rye and barley for a sweet and spicy flavor. Think Jim Beam, Evan Williams, Wild Turkey, Knob Creek, Booker's, Old Crow, Buffalo Trace, and Elijah Craig.

A rye bourbon is going to contain nearly 20 percent rye, dialing back on the corn and balancing the barley content similar to that of a traditional bourbon recipe. These bourbons are not as sweet and have a sort of back-of-the-tongue (you'll know it when you taste it) pepper spice. Think Basil Hayden's, Kentucky Tavern, Four Roses, Bulleit, Woodford Reserve, Old Forester, Old Grand-Dad, 1792, and Very Old Barton.

Wheat bourbons are similar to traditional bourbons with 70–80 percent corn, but they replace rye with wheat, allowing the sweetness of corn and the sugars from the barrel to come through. These bourbons are soft and sweet. Think Maker's Mark, W. L. Weller, Van Winkle, Rebel Yell, and Larceny.

4 | The First Distillery to Use the Steam-Powered Distillation Process

If you want to make bourbon, you're going to need a still. And while you can buy a small version on the internet—yes, seriously—Kentucky's most distinguished bourbon makers need something just a little bit bigger. Have you ever noticed the large, copper, genie-bottle-looking things on a distillery tour? Those are stills. And they're not just for photo ops.

Above: The continuous stills at Woodford Reserve Distillery in Versailles. Fermented mash is distilled in these to between 65 and 80 percent alcohol.

Kentucky bourbon makers agree that the first still likely came with the first settlers to Harrodsburg in 1774. The early still was built with a copper pot, a gooseneck, and a copper worm, or coil.

A still—whether a pot still or a continuous, or column, design—distills fermented mash into a clear spirit that bourbon insiders refer to as "White Dog," which becomes bourbon. *Still with us?* We'll break it down.

Bourbon starts with a grain mixture traditionally made up of 51 percent corn (legally required to call it bourbon) and the remaining 49 percent either rye, wheat, malted barley, or some combination of these. This is called the mash bill. The grains are mixed with water and usually, though not always, combined with mash from a previous distillation to ensure consistent pH levels across batches and protect flavor consistency. Yeast is then added, and the mash is fermented in large tanks. This fermented mash is then distilled to between 65 and 80 percent alcohol.

In the early years of bourbon making, mash was distilled using a pot still. These pot stills were heated directly, not through steam heat, and could only produce spirits in batches. Today, many distilleries use column stills, which allow for continuous distilling.

The Hope Distillery in Louisville is the first known distillery to experiment with steam-power distillation. It began using this new technology in 1816.

The distillery sat on one hundred acres in the present-day western Portland area of Louisville and had grain machinery that could do the work of several dozen men. Its stills were continuous—a novelty of its time—and heated by steam, which no other distillery was utilizing. The large, continuous stills changed the flavor of the bourbon, which made some consumers who were used to liquor made in smaller pot stills leery. It operated for a few years but was forced to close when it ran out of money. Despite its failure, Hope Distillery had the right idea. Less than fifty years later, most major distilleries had converted to steam power and continuous distilling.

The Peerless Distillery is on the Kentucky Bourbon Trail's Craft Tour. It sits on North Tenth Street in Louisville and houses a one-of-a-kind twenty-six-foot continuous copper still made in Louisville by Vendome Copper & Brass Works.

Check out the stills on your distillery tours. Each brand has a different style as unique as the recipe inside it, and stills are one of the more recognizable iconic parts of the distilling process.

A ROAD TRIP TO THE PEERLESS DISTILLERY ON THE KENTUCKY ★ BOURBON TRAIL'S CRAFT TOUR ★

According to *The Encyclopedia of Louisville*, the Hope Distillery used to sit at the intersection of Portland Avenue and Main Street—a junction that doesn't exist today. Even though the historic building doesn't stand today, roadtrippers can travel not too far from this site to the Peerless Distillery on North Tenth Street.

Kentucky Peerless Distilling got its start as Worsham Distilling Company in Henderson, Kentucky, in the early 1880s, but it was under the leadership of entrepreneur Henry Kraver that the distillery began operating under the Peerless name and production began to flourish. Kraver put the family's first bourbon into barrels in 1889, upgraded machinery, and invested in additional warehouses that complied with the federal Bottled-in-Bond Act of 1897. Production of Peerless whiskey increased substantially from eight to two hundred barrels a day. During Prohibition, Peerless was one of the few available liquors available by prescription for medicinal use.

Today, five generations are connected to Peerless Distilling, and the brand was revived by Henry Kraver's great-grandson Corky Taylor and his son, Carson. The Peerless Distillery is now one of the most automated distilleries in the state with cutting-edge technology and a state-of-the-art facility. Under one roof, the select Kentucky Peerless grains are milled, cooked, fermented, double distilled, and barreled as bourbon and rye whiskey. The facility houses a 2,500-gallon cooker, six fermentation tanks, a 3,800-gallon beer well, and a one-of-a-kind twenty-six-foot continuous copper still made in Louisville by Vendome Copper & Brass Works.

★ IF YOU GO   **Kentucky Peerless Distilling**

The historic distillery is located at 120 North Tenth Street in Louisville. It offers behind-the-scenes tours for an up-close look at how it crafts its bourbon from grain to bottle all under one roof. Learn more about tours at **kentuckypeerless.com /distillery-tour-louisville-kentucky**.

Peerless is on the Kentucky Bourbon Trail's Craft Distillery Tour. This tour winds through the rolling hills and Bluegrass fields deep into bourbon country to unveil the unrivaled craftsmanship of the Kentucky bourbon industry. This tour is designed for enthusiasts looking to experience Kentucky bourbon at its core, with opportunities to try new handcrafted brands from thirteen distilleries along the way.

Grab your bourbon passport and, in addition to Peerless, head to Barrel House Distilling Company and Bluegrass Distillers in

Lexington, Boone County Distilling Company in Independence, Corsair Distillery in Bowling Green, Hartfield & Company in Paris, Kentucky Artisan Distillery in Crestwood, Limestone Branch Distillery in Lebanon, MB Roland Distillery in Pembroke, New Riff Distillery in Newport, Old Pogue Distillery in Maysville (look for the Clooneys!), Wilderness Trail Distillery in Danville, and Willett Distillery in Bardstown.

Don't forget to do your research! Some of these microdistilleries have limited hours and tour times. Learn more at **kybourbon trail.com/craft-tour.**

Why Is Bourbon Stored in Barrels?

To be called Kentucky Straight Bourbon Whiskey, the liquor must be stored in a new charred oak barrel. It's an official rule that makes bourbon unique from other spirits. According to the Kentucky Distillers' Association, the earliest known mention of charring a barrel is in a letter from John Corlis, a Lexington grocer turned distiller, written in 1826. In his letter, Corlis orders more barrels of whiskey and suggests, "If the barrels burnt on the inside, say only a 16th of an inch, then the whiskey will be much improved."

A bourbon barrel at Woodford Reserve Distillery.

The recipe may be the soul of the bourbon, but the barrel and aging provide the unique flavors. How long it is aged, what type of warehouse it sits in, and the location of the barrels inside the rackhouse are all factors. Kentucky's seasons contribute greatly to the aging process. The state's cold winters cause the wood staves of the barrel to contract and draw the bourbon into their pores. Then, the long, hot, and humid summers allow the wood to expand and push the bourbon, which spent the winter months absorbing sugars and flavor from the wood, back into the barrel. Most distillers estimate that barrel aging is responsible for anywhere between 50 and 75 percent of the final flavor of a bourbon.

To be a bourbon, the liquor must enter the barrel for aging at no more than 125 proof. Different distillers age bourbon for different numbers of years, and since many of the best bourbons are aged for more than a decade, bourbon brands need a fairly expansive property to store numerous large barrels. You can imagine the challenge that this presents.

In 1879, Frederick Stitzel helped solve this bourbon conundrum when he patented a system of tiered storage racks that increased air circulation and made it easier to move the barrels when needed.

Today, Four Roses Bourbon in Lawrenceburg is the only distillery using single-story rack warehouses. They say it minimizes temperature variations, providing a gentle, undisturbed, and more stable aging process, resulting in bourbon with more consistent flavors, body, and aromas.

A ROAD TRIP TO
★ FOUR ROSES DISTILLERY ★

By now, we're sure you've realized that no story of a bourbon brand is complete without a complicated and widely debated history. Four Roses is no exception. In fact, this is perhaps one of the more unusual distillery histories out there.

The Four Roses logo adorns the unique Spanish mission-style architecture at the distillery in Lawrenceburg and has several tall tales about its origins.

We'll start at one of the beginnings.

By some accounts, the brand was founded by prominent Atlanta society member Rufus Mathewson Rose, a druggist who studied medicine and owned and operated the R. M. Rose & Company Distillery in Vining, Georgia. The story goes that Rose wanted to create a brand name for the whiskey coming out of the Kentucky distillery that he founded in the 1860s. Today, we may not consider branding a big deal—it's practically required in order to sell a product—but in the late 1800s, marketing was sort of a novel idea. His whiskey was already known as Rose's Whiskey, so the idea of using the image of a rose seemed practical. Here's where the story gets romanticized a bit. It's said that as Rose waffled on the final name of his Kentucky bourbon, his four daughters showed up to one of the family's frequent formal balls, each with roses for their corsages. When the girls appeared at the top of the stairs with their flowers, proud papa decided that he would name his new brand Four Roses.

We kind of love this story. What could be better than a historic brand created by a father and named for his daughters? But while we like the story, there are a few hiccups—the biggest one being that Rufus Mathewson Rose of Atlanta only had one daughter. And a son.

Today, the operators of Four Roses Distillery in Lawrenceburg don't credit Rose for founding the brand or the brick-and-mortar where it's made. According to the astute tour guides, business-man Paul Jones Jr. moved to Louisville and opened an office in a section of historic Main Street called Whiskey Row. Four years later, he trademarked the name Four Roses. His romantic story—and the version the distillery sticks to—begins when Jones became smitten by the beauty of a Southern belle. He sent her a proposal, and she replied that if she were to answer yes, she would wear a corsage of roses on her gown to the upcoming ball. Of course, when she arrived in her beautiful gown, she wore four red roses, and Jones named his bourbon Four Roses as a symbol of his devout passion for the lovely belle. And of course, they lived happily ever after.

There are questions about this version, too, however. Some historical articles give Paul Jones credit for operating Four Roses from the end of Prohibition until he sold it to Seagram's in 1941, but there are no records to indicate that Jones ever married. Maybe she said no after all.

Want to know what we think? The *My Old Kentucky Road Trip* theory goes something like this: The R. M. Rose Distilling Company of Atlanta, which later established distilleries in Chattanooga, Tennessee, and Lawrenceburg, Kentucky, was owned and operated through two generations by Rufus M. Rose, his brother Origen Rose, and their two sons, thus representing the four roses. Pretty boring, huh?

We're not sure the name is even the most confusing part of the history of Four Roses Bourbon. Despite the great success the brand experienced in the 1930s, 1940s, and 1950s, parent company Seagram's (which purchased operations in 1943 from Paul Jones) decided to discontinue the sale of Kentucky Straight Bourbon in the United States and moved it into the rapidly grow-ing Asian and European markets. Back at home, Four Roses sold

Visitors tour the unique single-story rackhouses at Four Roses in Cox's Creek. Stacking barrels just six high allows for a more consistent aging process. It is the only distillery to use these single-story warehouses.

a blended whiskey, meaning it was mostly neutral spirits with only a small amount of whiskey added for flavor.

To Kentuckians, it just seems wrong that the company would choose to stop selling Kentucky bourbon in Kentucky. But despite not being available in the United States, Four Roses straight bourbon whiskey quickly became the top-selling bourbon in Europe and Japan (and it retains that title today). In 1966, Jim Rutledge began working with then distillery owner Seagram's to craft Four Roses bourbon in Kentucky again, and after long, tireless years working to restore the brand to its roots, the Kirin Brewery Company purchased the distillery in 2002 and once again began selling Kentucky Straight Bourbon Whiskey in the United States. Rutledge was its Master Distiller until he retired in 2015.

Today, Four Roses continues to be a leader in the bourbon market and no longer produces or sells blended whiskey.

Remember those barrel rackhouses we were going on about? Any distillery in Kentucky will give you a great view of Frederick Stitzel's tiered bourbon storage racks. But travel to Lawrenceburg, twenty-two miles south of Frankfort, to see Four Roses' single-story rack warehouses along the banks of Cox Creek.

Guests can tour Four Roses' warehouse and bottling facility to see firsthand how the bourbon is stored and bottled. Tours meet in the new 2,500-square-foot visitor center that features antique bottles, vintage advertising, and other memorabilia. To learn more about the history of Four Roses, visit **fourroses bourbon.com**. The visitor center is located at 624 Lotus Road in Cox's Creek.

5 | The First Bourbon to Be Bottled and Sealed for Sale

With so many distilleries producing countless brands across Kentucky, many consumers identify their favorite brands based on the shape, size, and branding of its bottle. And while that may seem more marketing than good bourbon making, the history of packaging is actually rather important.

In 1870, George Garvin Brown, a pharmaceutical salesman turned bourbon merchant, recognized that bottling bourbon in consistent packaging not only gave his product legitimacy but

Above: Old Forester is produced by Brown-Forman. Visit the company's headquarters in Louisville to see a water tower shaped like the Old Forester bottle.

also discouraged tampering and boasted safety to consumers. Old Forrester (spelled Old Forester today), named for Union army surgeon Dr. William Forrester, was the first bourbon to be exclusively sold by the bottle.

In the early days, Old Forester was sold in pharmacies as a medicinal product—one of just six brands allowed to produce liquor during Prohibition. The brand is thought to be the only bourbon continually distilled and marketed by the founding family before, during, and after Prohibition.

In 1904, the automatic bottling system was patented, making it possible to produce four bottles per second inexpensively and with uniform quality. This invention helped make bottling bourbon routine. Today, more than one hundred thousand cases of Old Forester leave the Brown-Forman distillery in Shively each year.

A ROAD TRIP TO
★ LOUISVILLE'S WHISKEY ROW ★

Whiskey Row is a block of historic buildings stretching between 101 and 133 West Main Street in downtown Louisville. The buildings include the famous House of Weller (121 West Main), the Trade Mart Building (131 West Main), and J.T.S. Brown and Son's Complex (105–109 West Main). This stretch of history once served as home to the bourbon industry in Louisville, built between 1852 and 1905. Around 2011, this block was slated for demolition, but preservationists and local developers partnered with the City of Louisville to save these bourbon bones and create Whiskey Row.

Once home to more than fifty active distilleries, this block between First and Second Streets is still under construction and has been plagued by challenges, including a 2015 fire that burned down three buildings. But when it is fully developed, the block will feature a distillery tourist attraction, two upscale hotels, and a major retail outlet.

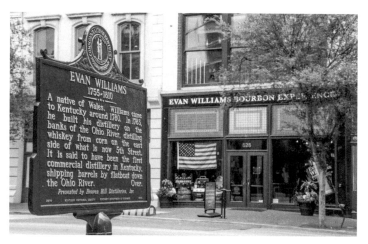

Whiskey Row in Louisville is a block of historic buildings stretching between 101 and 133 West Main Street that once served as home to the bourbon industry in Louisville. Today, Whiskey Row celebrates its history as new bourbon tourist attractions are opening to whiskey drinkers.

★ IF YOU GO Louisville's Whiskey Row and Urban Bourbon Trail

Make sure you grab your Urban Bourbon Trail passport before you visit to earn your status as an official bourbon country citizen. Don't miss the Evan Williams Bourbon Experience or Brown-Forman's Old Forester tourism experience, featuring a welcome area, fermentation room, cooperage, tasting room, and bottling line.

While you're in town, stop by the Old Seelbach Bar in the Seelbach Hilton. Located at 500 South Fourth Street, the Seelbach hotel has hosted gangsters, politicians, and celebrities for generations. It is listed on the National Register of Historic Places, and it is said that the Seelbach served as F. Scott Fitzgerald's inspiration for *The Great Gatsby* (Daisy Buchanan was from Louisville, after all). The hotel's Oakroom restaurant was a favorite hangout of Al Capone.

Learn more about other stops along the Urban Bourbon Trail at **www.bourboncountry.com/things-to-do/urban-bourbon-trail**.

A ROAD TRIP TO
REBECCA RUTH CANDY TO TASTE
★ THE ORIGINAL BOURBON BALL ★

Rebecca Ruth Candy was founded in Frankfort in 1919 by two substitute school teachers, Ruth Hanly and Rebecca Gooch. Each holiday season, they would make chocolates for friends and family, and after years of praise, they decided they were better candy makers than substitute teachers. Not many women went into business in the early twentieth century, but Rebecca and Ruth rented the barroom at the Frankfort Hotel (which had been closed by Prohibition) and began making chocolates on a twelve-foot marble table.

The table became iconic for the candy company. Ruth purchased the marble slab, which was originally a bar top in the Old Capitol Hotel dating back to around 1850, in 1917 for $10. Eventually, the table was named "Edna's Table" after an employee who worked for Rebecca Ruth Candy for sixty-seven years before retiring at age ninety.

Bourbon balls sit in a case at Rebecca Ruth Candy in Frankfort. Founded in 1919, the candy company claims to have invented the original bourbon ball.

Rebecca Ruth Candy was a great success, but it is perhaps most famous for inventing a unique and distinctively Kentucky candy called the bourbon ball. You can find bourbon balls across the country now. Ruth originally got the idea for mixing up a sugary bourbon filling at Frankfort's sesquicentennial celebration in 1936 on the suggestion of dignitary Eleanor Hume Offutt. Ruth worked on the recipe for two years before perfecting the still-secret process.

Life wasn't always easy for the women—Ruth lost her husband, the Great Depression settled over Frankfort, and a large part of the candy factory was destroyed by fire—but they never gave up. Rebecca ended up selling her share of the business to Ruth, and in 1964, Ruth retired, leaving the business to her son, John. Today, John runs the business with his son, Charles.

★ IF YOU GO ▸ Rebecca Ruth Candy Factory

The candy factory is open to tours daily at its location just blocks from the Capitol building in Frankfort. Tour highlights include seeing Edna's Table and an antique candy furnace with hand-stirred copper kettles still in use today. The factory is located at 116 East Second Street in Frankfort. Learn more at **rebeccaruth .com**.

The Famous Mint Julep and How to Drink Bourbon Like a Kentuckian

While the mint julep can certainly be found at bars and derby parties outside of Kentucky, it is at its best in the Bluegrass State. It is a cocktail traditionally composed of bourbon, sugar, water, and mint, and it has been a Kentucky favorite since before horses were running the track at the famous Churchill Downs in Louisville. As early as 1816, silver julep cups were given as prizes at county fairs across Kentucky, and if you go back even further, a similar julep recipe was prescribed for stomach problems and sore throats.

Kentucky's famous mint julep brings two Kentucky traditions—horses and bourbon—together at Churchill Downs for the derby each year.

Perhaps our favorite thing about the mint julep is that it brings two famous Kentucky traditions together: horses and bourbon. It is widely believed that Meriwether Lewis Clark Jr., the founder of the Louisville Jockey Club, builder of Churchill Downs, and founder of the Kentucky Derby, actually planted mint for cocktails around the clubhouse when the track was first built in 1875. And while the mint julep has been the traditional beverage of Churchill Downs for almost a century, it wasn't declared the official derby drink until 1938.

Each year, almost 120,000 mint juleps are served over the two-day period of the Kentucky Oaks and the Kentucky Derby at Churchill Downs alone. This requires more than ten thousand bottles of bourbon, one thousand pounds of freshly harvested mint, and sixty thousand pounds of ice. Scale that down a bit for your next house party. You'll only need a julep cup of shaved ice, Kentucky bourbon, some homemade simple syrup (boil two cups of water and two cups of sugar together for five minutes), and a sprig of fresh mint.

Until recently, a bit of controversy surrounded Churchill's mint julep recipe. For nearly two decades, bartenders at the track used Early Times Kentucky whiskey as the liquor component of the cocktail. Do you know the problem with that? Early Times isn't officially bourbon. You see, one of the mandates for bourbon is that the whiskey is aged in new charred oak barrels. Early Times is stored in used barrels—a big bourbon no-no. But let's not dwell on the past. These days, derby goers proudly drink Old Forester *bourbon* in their mint juleps. Let's all breathe a collective sigh of relief.

Of course, any true Kentuckian will tell you that he or she drinks bourbon "neat." That means plain, in a glass with nothing else, simple, flavorful—as it was meant to be enjoyed. Many toss in a couple of ice cubes or a splash of cola. Others explore a bit of mixology. If you want to get creative, try your bourbon with a little bit of Ale-8-One. This unique ginger soda is made in Winchester and complements bourbon on ice. Here's one of our very favorite bourbon recipes:

Classic Old-Fashioned

(the hard way and the easy way)

Place a sugar cube in the bottom of an old-fashioned glass (or you can put a teaspoon of sugar in a thick-bottomed cocktail glass of your choosing).

Moisten the sugar with a few dashes of Angostura bitters. It is very easy to find bitters at just about any store that sells beverages. For a bit more flavor, a lot of folks like to muddle a wedge of orange and a maraschino cherry in the bottom of a glass with the sugar and bitters, then add the other ingredients. If you don't have a muddler, the back of a spoon works great to crush some of the flavor from the fruit.

Drop in a few ice cubes and a splash of hot water or soda water and stir with a bar spoon (or a regular spoon; no need to get fancy on our account). Add bourbon. The precise bartender would call for two ounces. We call for whatever makes you happy and is to your taste.

Bottoms up!

★ HELPFUL LINKS ★

Heaven Hill Distillery **www.heavenhill.com**
Maker's Mark Distillery **www.makersmark.com**
Castle and Key Distillery **castleandkey.com**
The Kentucky Bourbon Trail **kybourbontrail.com**
Kentucky Bourbon Whiskey: An American Heritage by Michael
    Veach: available from your favorite bookseller, or **www**
    .kentuckypress.com
The Encyclopedia of Louisville by John E. Kleber: available from
    your favorite bookseller, or **www.kentuckypress.com**
The Atlantic **www.theatlantic.com/business/archive**
    /2015/05/women-making-whiskey-an-800-year
    -history/393260/
The Kentucky Legislature **www.lrc.ky.gov/record**
    /Moments15RS/web/legislative%20moment%2015.pdf;
    www.lrc.ky.gov/record/Moments06RS/25_web_leg
    _moments.htm
Liberty, Kentucky **www.libertykentucky.org**
Lexington Herald-Leader **www.kentucky.com/news**
    /business/bourbon-industry/article44509929.html
Author Fred Minnick's blog **www.fredminnick.com/2014**
    /09/12/one-proud-author-makers-marks-first-lady
    -enters-bourbon-hall-fame/
Louisville Courier-Journal **www.courier-journal.com/story**
    /news/history/river-city-retro/2014/11/14
    /celebrating-history-jefferson-bourbon/19022425/

Part Two
KENTUCKY'S RIVER TOWNS

Many say that the secret to bourbon is all in the recipe: limestone-filtered water, indigenous corn, and four seasons through the year that aid in the barrel-aging process. But the real secret to bourbon's success snakes across Kentucky's northern and western borders.

The Ohio and Mississippi Rivers were instrumental to the growth and prosperity of Kentucky's bourbon industry. Without the broad, swift shipping routes close at hand, bourbon might have never made it across the borders of the Bluegrass State to become America's native spirit.

Today, the river towns continue to play an important role in the state's economy as ports of trade and tourism. You might not want to swim from Catlettsburg in the east to the Kentucky Bend in the west, but if you did sail along Kentucky's river borders, you'd follow the same route that the state's earliest bourbon magnates used to distribute their wares across the country and, eventually, around the globe.

These days, the same trip can be accomplished via the far more accessible US and Kentucky interstate systems. Though, if you're inclined to grab a barrel and attempt to float your way across the state, be warned—these are no lazy rivers. As the largest tributary of the mighty Mississippi, the Ohio River discharges almost 32,000 cubic feet of water per second at the Falls of the Ohio in Louisville.

6 | Louisville

A ROAD TRIP TO
★ THE FALLS OF THE OHIO ★

In the growing American economy of the eighteenth and nineteenth centuries, bourbon boomed. Then, as now, the only place to get the best bourbon was in Kentucky. But Kentucky distillers had a problem: geography. To the east, mountains made shipping a difficult chore, and travel by land was still no easy task.

Above: Louisville's skyline captured from across the Ohio River at the Falls of the Ohio State Park in Indiana.

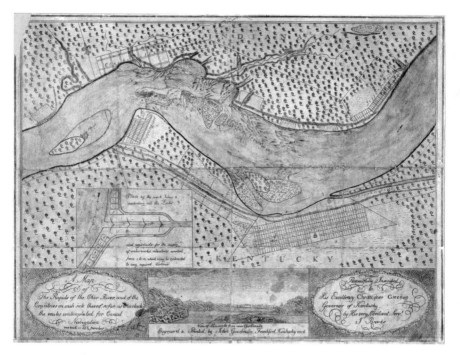

Brooks, J., and John Goodman. *A map of the rapids of the Ohio River and of the countries on each side thereof: so far, as to include the routes contemplated for canal navigation.* Frankfort, Ky.: Engrav'd & printed by John Goodman, 1806. Map. Retrieved from the Library of Congress, www.loc.gov/item/96687584/. (Accessed November 7, 2017.)

Before railroads began to cut across the country, the best way to export goods was via water. In this, Kentucky was fortunate—the Mississippi River was a profitable pathway to the northern and southern states as well as the Port of New Orleans, and the Ohio River enabled shipments to travel east to Pittsburgh and the Atlantic states and west to meet with the mighty Mississippi. It was an ideal situation for the bourbon distillers whose elixirs were already a point of pride in the culture of the state.

In the 981 miles of its length, the Ohio River only has one navigational barrier: the Falls of the Ohio in Louisville, Kentucky. Any flatboats or steamboats that wanted to sail past Louisville had to first unload their passengers and cargoes before they could float across the twenty-six-foot drop in the river. Until the Louisville and Portland Canal Company built a canal in 1830 to bypass the two-mile-long impediment, travel and shipping were delayed by the falls. Louisville's nickname, "Falls City," comes from the city's growth as one of the first cities west of the Appalachian Mountains, thanks to the portage over the falls.

The falls were a natural stopping point for pioneers and the American militiamen of the Revolutionary War—including Louisville founder George Rogers Clark. Clark's company alighted at a small island above the falls that they named Corn Island, in honor of the first crop planted there. It's not hard to imagine that their crop found its way into a few barrels of whiskey distilled on-site as well.

As Clark's outpost grew from a camp to a fort to a bustling river city, commerce grew up around the falls' natural stopping point in the Ohio River. With the construction of the Louisville and Portland Canal in 1830, the Falls of the Ohio were no longer an impediment to shipping traffic along the river. Today, the Louisville and Portland Canal (renamed the McAlpine Locks and Dam by the Army Corps of Engineers) still serves as the only point of passage over the Falls of the Ohio and includes a hydroelectric dam that, quite literally, helps power the city of Louisville.

As the Industrial Revolution took off, steamboats began sailing through with more regularity, and commercial distillers took over production in the state. Kentucky's first steam-powered commercial distillery—the Hope Distillery—was built in Louisville's Portland neighborhood, west of downtown, in 1816. Though it was considered a massive failure and closed within three years, the Hope Distillery helped usher in a revolution in Kentucky's bourbon industry.

Steam power brought not only steamboats but also trains. Kentucky's first railroad, the Lexington and Ohio Railroad, was meant to connect Lexington and Frankfort with the Falls of the Ohio but was never completed. It did, however, help lay the track for one of the most successful shipping enterprises in American history—the Louisville and Nashville Railroad (L&N). You may have heard of the L&N via Jean Ritchie's song "The L&N Don't

The Falls of the Ohio along the Ohio River at Louisville. While a Kentucky treasure, this natural wonder is best accessed at the state park located in Clarksville, Indiana.

Stop Here Anymore." The L&N operated for more than 130 years, expanding its rail lines across the South. You can see evidence of its success in Union Station on West Broadway in Louisville— now home to the Transit Authority of River City.

From Kentucky's earliest days to the first locomotive on the L&N in 1855, the waterways were the only efficient way to move Kentucky's native product to consumers. As trains continued to crisscross the state throughout the nineteenth and twentieth centuries, rails converged on Falls City, bringing commercially produced bourbon from all areas of the state to ship out from Louisville. The Louisville wharf, already a key marketplace, became the center of the big business of bourbon in Kentucky.

★ IF YOU GO Falls of the Ohio

The modern-day falls are still an excellent spot for exploration, sightseeing, and shipping traffic. Despite the state park's location in Clarksville, Indiana, across the river, the falls are still claimed by Kentucky. The state park not only marks the site where Meriwether Lewis and William Clark (George Rogers Clark's brother) met before their famous expedition to the Pacific Ocean but is also one of the largest exposed Devonian fossil beds in the world. (By the way, the Devonian period is also known as the "Age of Fish" in the Paleozoic era, thanks to the rich diversity evolving in Earth's waterways.) If you're into fossil hunting, be warned, these fossils are "look, don't touch!" But, if you stop by the park in the autumn, the river will be at its lowest point, exposing more of the fossil bed.

You can also learn more about the natural history of the Falls of the Ohio in the park's Interpretive Center, or explore on your own with a hike or a picnic. For the true Kentucky history buff, make an appointment to visit George Rogers Clark's cabin, which he built as an escape and to live independently from his sister at Locust Grove.

If you're interested in a view of the falls from the Kentucky side of the river, the Louisville Riverwalk is your best trail—offering excellent views of the McAlpine Locks and Dam, where you can watch the coal barges and other boats navigate the falls. Parking is available at Lannan Park in Louisville's Portland neighborhood, next to the canal.

HOW A RIVER HELPED MAKE
★ BOURBON A HOUSEHOLD NAME ★

We've already told the story: bourbon got its name from Bourbon County, Kentucky, which had been named for the royal House of Bourbon in France. But how did bourbon come to conquer the US liquor market and eventually the world? As Don Draper definitely didn't say, "What you call love was invented by guys like me to sell . . . bourbon."

According to Michael R. Veach, bourbon historian at the Filson Historical Society, bourbon's commercial success probably came about as a result of a fortuitous shipwreck at the Falls of the

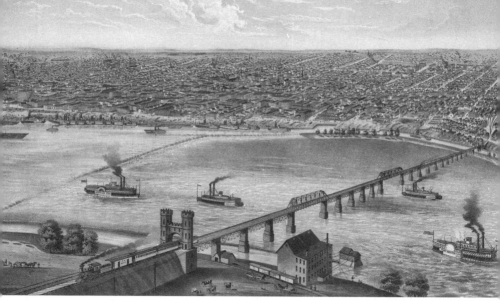

Ruger, A., Charles Shober & Co, and Chicago Lithographing Co. *Bird's eye view of Louisville, Kentucky 1876*. [Chicago, 1876] Map. Retrieved from the Library of Congress, www.loc.gov/item/73693416/. (Accessed November 7, 2017.)

Ohio and good branding. His book, *Kentucky Bourbon Whiskey*, posits the Tarascon brothers, Louis and John, as the masterminds of bourbon.

Unaged whiskey had been traded across the Ohio River and up and down the Mississippi since the earliest days of American history. The clear liquor, less appealing than its aged, amber-colored counterpart, was not especially profitable for distillers. Many, in the bustling Port of New Orleans especially, preferred aged liquors like brandy and cognac.

The Tarascon brothers, who had fled France during the Reign of Terror, established a shipyard in their new American home in Philadelphia. After losing a ship at the Falls of the Ohio, the brothers established a warehouse nearby and continued to trade with New Orleans. Seeking better profits, the brothers were ideally situated to purchase, age, and resell the darker-colored whiskey to the New Orleanians, who probably appreciated a tipple that paid homage to the glory days of France before the revolution as well as a libation that cost less than brandy and cognac.

MASTER OF BOURBON AND
★ MASTER OF THE WHARF ★

One of the newest features on Louisville's Whiskey Row, the Evan Williams Experience, honors the legacy and contributions of one of the earliest distillers in Kentucky's history. Williams immigrated to Louisville in the 1780s and built a whiskey distillery on the banks of the Ohio River—one of the earliest commercial distilleries in the state—and began shipping his bourbon by flatboat down the Ohio River.

Williams's business acumen and stature in the community led to his election to the Louisville Board of Trustees, where he was said to bring a bottle of bourbon to every meeting. The growing city of Louisville was beginning to realize the importance of the port and the crucial role it played in assisting portage over the Falls of the Ohio. In 1797, Evan Williams was elected the first wharf master of the City of Louisville. As wharf master, he ensured that the small harbor remained uncrowded and that all boats were unloaded and moved within forty-eight hours of their arrival—a huge responsibility for what was to become one of the largest inland ports in the United States.

A ROAD TRIP TO THE
★ US MARINE HOSPITAL ★

Situated near the Falls of the Ohio in Louisville's historic Portland neighborhood, the US Marine Hospital is a marvel of history and survival. Though the name might suggest otherwise, the hospital was unaffiliated with the military and was built to care for sick and injured boatmen of America's western waterways.

Sailing and navigating in the nineteenth century was not the easiest or the safest occupation. The boat- and seamen were treated for injuries from wrecks, mishandling freight, and even engine and boiler explosions. They contracted diseases like cholera, smallpox, and yellow fever. And, according to the neighborhood

Louisville's historic Marine Hospital located in the city's Portland neighborhood. The hospital was built in the nineteenth century to care for sick and injured boatmen of America's western waterways.

association Portland Now, Inc., sailors who were docked in the port towns lived a rough-and-tumble life, where violence, alcoholism, and venereal diseases sent them to the hospital.

Prior to the Civil War, the Marine Hospital Service withheld twenty cents from merchant seamen's paychecks to fund hospitals at various ports across the country, which also received funds from the federal government—establishing the first publicly funded health care and prepaid insurance in the United States. The Louisville Marine Hospital is the only one of these hospitals still standing—even after surviving two tornadoes—and is considered the best remaining antebellum hospital in the country by the National Park Service.

The Marine Hospital stands today looking much as it did after it was built in the middle of the nineteenth century, having been carefully restored by the City of Louisville with help from the Army Corps of Engineers. Even if you're not making a stop in Portland to gaze at the falls, you'll still notice the hospital's antebellum architecture as you make your way through West Louisville on Interstate 64.

The US Marine Hospital is more of a "look, but don't touch" destination. You can easily see the antebellum building as you drive east on Interstate 64 from New Albany, Indiana. But, pull off into the Portland neighborhood, and you can park on the grounds of the nearby health center to walk around.

You can also hike around Lannan Park along the interstate for views of both the falls and the Marine Hospital. If you're in great shape, the Louisville Riverwalk will take you from Portland at Northwestern Parkway and North Thirty-First Street all the way to Butchertown—more than eight miles away!

★ HELPFUL LINKS ★

Falls of the Ohio   **www.fallsoftheohio.org**
Historic Portland   **www.portlandlouisville.com**
Louisville Waterfront Park   **louisvillewaterfront.com**
L&N Historical Society   **www.lnrr.org**

7 | Maysville

★ THE ORIGINAL BOURBON COUNTY ★

Before Kentucky was Kentucky, Kentucky was Virginia. Nearly everything northeast of Lexington was established as Bourbon County, Virginia, just after the American Revolution. Of course, it was this same revolutionary spirit that drove Virginia's westernmost citizens to ask for their independence. First, it was an arduous task to travel from early Kentucky to the Virginia state

Above: The Ohio River from Maysville. A major port on the Ohio River, this town's early growth enabled distillers to capitalize.

65

capital, and second, Virginia did not allow its western citizens to trade with the French port of New Orleans. Kentucky finally did gain its statehood in 1792, with Isaac Shelby elected as its first governor.

With its statehood established and fewer attacks by the local Native American tribes after the conclusion of the Northwest Indian War, the fifteenth state in the Union began to grow and flourish. Nowhere was this more evident than in Maysville, a geographically strategic point on the Ohio River. Along an old buffalo trail, or trace, westward, Maysville was originally founded as Kenton's Station by frontiersman Simon Kenton. The river landing near Kenton's Station was known as Limestone, and Limestone was destined to become one of the biggest early names in bourbon.

Maysville, with its Limestone Landing, quickly became one of the most important port cities in Kentucky. It became an entry point for much of the river traffic headed from Pittsburgh to the Ohio River and on to the Mississippi. The town's early growth enabled distillers to capitalize.

The earliest distilleries in Maysville marketed their bourbons as "Old Bourbon County Whisky." Even the rye farmers of Pennsylvania and Maryland who distilled their own rye whiskeys shipped their barrels through Maysville. Historian Henry G. Crowgey found the first official advertisement for "Bourbon Whiskey," placed by Maysville firm Stout & Adams in 1821. But Limestone Landing had made its name much earlier.

Perhaps the most popular explanation for how bourbon got its name is thanks to the earliest shipments from Maysville to New Orleans. It is said that the barrels that came from "Limestone, Bourbon County, Kentucky" were the best sellers. Customers began to ask for that Bourbon County whiskey by name, and soon enough, bourbon whiskey became the booming market it is today. Historians since have poked plenty of holes in this tale, but it is fun to imagine the early revelers of Bourbon Street sipping Kentucky bourbon.

Vintage Old Pogue label. Courtesy of The Old Pogue Distillery, LLC.

A ROAD TRIP TO
★ OLD POGUE DISTILLERY ★

Though Maysville's bourbon history dried up somewhat following Prohibition, whiskey is flowing in Mason County once again thanks to the Pogue family.

Henry Edgar Pogue had been working as chief distiller for O. H. P. Thomas in Maysville after the Civil War, and in 1876, Pogue bought out his former boss. Pogue opened his own distillery, making older brands, such as Old Time and Old Maysville Club, as well as his own new ones. According to a newspaper article from the summer Pogue's distillery opened, he was making around ten barrels a day and utilizing a new copper boiler, "which affords all the advantages and none of the defects of the apparatus employed in making the best grades of Kentucky liquors" (*ExploreKYHistory*).

By the end of the century, Pogue was distilling fifty barrels a day, and the family brand was growing under Henry Pogue II. Unfortunately, Prohibition swept in, ending production despite the best efforts of Henry Pogue III to continue distributing "medicinal whiskey."

Today, Old Pogue distilling has reopened for business under the care of the fifth and sixth generations of the Pogue family. They continue to bottle and distribute their flagship tipple, Old Pogue Bourbon, as well as their original recipe for Old Maysville Club Rye Malt Whiskey.

★ IF YOU GO   Old Pogue Distillery

You'll have to make an appointment, but you can still visit the distillery on the same site as the historic H. E. Pogue Distillery. You can easily book a distillery tour via the Old Pogue website or by reaching out to the distillery directly. Tours are offered Thursday through Sunday and will earn you a stamp in your Kentucky Bourbon Trail Craft Tour passport.

To get there, you'll want to follow US 68, which was, at one point, designated the Maysville Road. If you're really dedicated, you can take US 68 all the way from Reidland, Kentucky, in McCracken County, to Maysville and onward into northwest Ohio.

Elsewhere in Maysville, be sure to lay a penny at Rosemary Clooney's grave in homage of the hometown girl's song, "If Teardrops Were Pennies."

Harriet Beecher Stowe, 1811 to 1896. ca. 1880. Photograph. Retrieved from the Library of Congress, www.loc.gov /item/2004672776/. (Accessed November 7, 2017.)

PAY HOMAGE AT THE
HARRIET BEECHER STOWE,
★ SLAVERY TO FREEDOM MUSEUM ★

Annexed by Maysville in the nineteenth century, the neighborhood known as Old Washington was one of the earliest settlements in Kentucky with several claims to fame. Washington is thought to be the first town in the United States named for President George Washington; its early residents were mainly veterans of the Revolutionary War. A name like Washington is a heavy reputation to live up to, but it was a not-yet famous visitor in 1833 who would provide one of the town's most enduring legacies.

Harriet Beecher was a teacher at the Western Female Institute in Cincinnati when she came to Washington, Kentucky, to visit a student. It was on this trip that Beecher witnessed a slave auction in front of Washington's courthouse that would help inspire her to write *Uncle Tom's Cabin*. It is said she found the characters of Topsy and Uncle Tom on her visit to Washington, Kentucky. When he met the famous author later in her life, Abraham Lincoln remarked, "So this is the little lady who started the big war."

Harriet Beecher, who became Harriet Beecher Stowe, was an active abolitionist in Cincinnati, and her family supported the Underground Railroad and hosted a safe house along the route.

In Old Washington, the Marshall Key House, now known as the Harriet Beecher Stowe, Slavery to Freedom Museum, was the home of Stowe's student, Elizabeth Marshall Key, who hosted her visit to Kentucky. The house is included on Maysville's Underground Railroad Tour and honors Stowe's contributions to the abolition of slavery.

Nearby, make a stop at the Paxton Inn, a station on the Underground Railroad. A hidden stairway between the first and second floors was used to hide runaway slaves until they could make their way to the safety of Ohio, a nonslaveholding state.

★ HELPFUL LINKS ★

City of Maysville, Kentucky   **www.cityofmaysville.com**
Old Pogue Distillery   **www.oldpogue.com**
City of Washington, Kentucky   **www.washingtonky.com**
Harriet Beecher Stowe Center   **www.harrietbeecher stowecenter.org**
Freedom Time Underground Railroad Tours   **freedom undergroundrailroad.com**
KET Education, Kentucky's Underground Railroad—
   Passage to Freedom   **www.ket.org/education/resources /kentuckys-underground-railroad-passage-freedom**
Tim Talbott. "H. E. Pogue Distillery." *ExploreKYHistory*: **http://explorekyhistory.ky.gov/items/show/421**. (Accessed December 28, 2017.)

8 | The Jackson Purchase

A ROAD TRIP TO PADUCAH FOR A
★ WHISKEY PARADE ★

While most think the Bluegrass and Knobs regions of Kentucky have the most bourbon-soaked history, western Kentucky also has its share of whiskey-provoked rabble-rousing, including unruly processionals. And if asked to which moment in Kentucky

Above: Constructed after a devastating flood in 1937, the floodwalls of Paducah in western Kentucky include fifty murals painted by Robert Dafford that depict the town's history.

history you might like to travel, a whiskey parade doesn't seem like a bad choice. What does a parade have to do with the history of bourbon? Glad you asked!

Thanks to the diligent research of the folks at the McCracken County Public Library, we know that the first commercial distillery on record in Paducah was the Old Terrell Distillery, which started selling whiskey at ten cents a glass in 1903. However, the temperance movement was nearing a new law to declare the production, transport, and sale of alcohol illegal.

In response to the protesters of the Anti-Saloon League, the Old Terrell Distillery staged whiskey parades in front of their offices on Jefferson Street with banners and music and, of course, bourbon. One December, the protesters were so angered by one of Terrell's whiskey parades that they attacked the march, smashing bottles of whiskey in their assault. Undiscouraged, the Terrells hosted another parade the very next day, Christmas Eve, with one of the founders as drum major, holding a pickaxe instead of a baton.

In the end, the temperance movement got what it wanted and the Old Terrell Distillery was forced to close. But today, distilleries are in operation in Paducah again, brewing bourbon and moonshine and keeping western Kentucky's whiskey tradition alive.

★ IF YOU GO Paducah

We haven't heard of any modern-day whiskey parades—call us if anyone finds a suggestion box in Paducah—but Paducah is full of great stops for the roadtripper with a designated driver in tow.

Follow the route of Terrell's whiskey parades from the nearby Moonshine Company down Jefferson Street, straight to downtown Paducah. Stop for a draught at Paducah Beer Werks on the way, or detour to Silent Brigade Distillery on your walk toward the river. If you're in need of a meal to balance your drink, we recommend a steak at Doe's Eat Place or something sweet from Kirchhoff's Bakery and Deli; both are *legendary* among the hometown crowd.

★ THE PADUCAH FLOODWALL★

When you live near a river—especially a river as wide and powerful as the Ohio or the Mississippi—precautions must be taken. For most river cities, this includes a floodwall. Along the Ohio River, floodwalls are used to protect cities from Huntington, West Virginia, to Louisville to Paducah.

Paducah constructed its floodwall after a devastating flood in 1937, when the waters of the Ohio River rose to almost sixty-one feet! You can see flood markers around town today that show how high the waters rose. After the flood, the US Army Corps of Engineers stepped in and erected the fourteen-foot-high edifice that protects the city. Why fourteen feet? It's the same height as the 1937 floodwaters, plus an extra three feet, just to be safe.

Why do you want to visit Paducah's floodwall today? For the fifty murals painted by Robert Dafford that stretch across the faces of the wall, depicting Paducah's history. Get in touch with the folks at Paducah Main Street to set up a guided tour while you're in town, or browse the art and read the descriptive plaque on your own self-guided stroll down the riverwalk.

IRVIN S. COBB AND THE ★ FIGHT AGAINST PROHIBITION★

Celebrated writer, humorist, and larger-than-life wit, the so-called duke of Paducah Irvin S. Cobb is one of Paducah's—and Kentucky's—favorite sons. At the height of his career, Cobb worked for Joseph Pulitzer's *New York World* as the highest paid staff reporter in the country. Despite his problematic opinions about people of other genders, races, and creeds (an unfortunate product of the time), Cobb can be praised for his contributions to the fight to repeal Prohibition.

The Association against the Prohibition Amendment was an active national organization fighting the good fight against the Eighteenth Amendment, and as chairman of the Authors

Irvin S. Cobb, bust portrait. ca. 1914. Photograph. Retrieved from the Library of Congress, www.loc.gov/item/2005685624/. (Accessed November 7, 2017.)

and Artists Committee, Cobb helped the cause by writing press releases and anti-Prohibition commentary. "If Prohibition is a noble experiment," he once said, "then the San Francisco fire and the Galveston flood should be listed among the noble experiments of our national history" (Ellis, 2017).

When Prohibition finally ended with the Twenty-First Amendment in 1933, Frankfort Distillery, one of six distilleries that were allowed to remain open during prohibition for

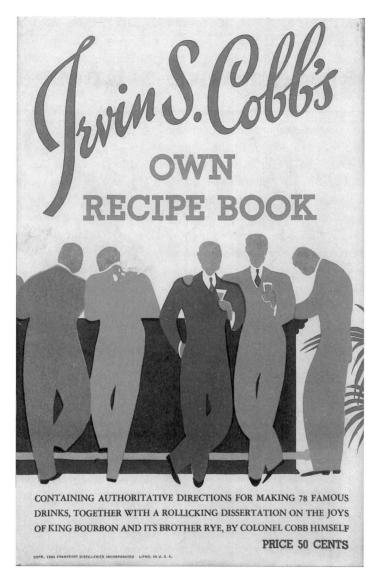

CONTAINING AUTHORITATIVE DIRECTIONS FOR MAKING 78 FAMOUS
DRINKS, TOGETHER WITH A ROLLICKING DISSERTATION ON THE JOYS
OF KING BOURBON AND ITS BROTHER RYE, BY COLONEL COBB HIMSELF

PRICE 50 CENTS

The cover of *Irvin Cobb's Own Recipe Book*, commissioned by Frankfort
Distillery in 1934.

medicinal purposes, asked Cobb to write a cocktail book to help reeducate Americans who had forgotten how to make great drinks. *Irvin Cobb's Own Recipe Book, Containing Authoritative Directions for Making 71 Famous Drinks, Together with a Rollicking Dissertation of the Joys of King Bourbon and Its Brother Rye, by Colonel Cobb Himself* contains recipes of Cobb's favorite (and not-so-favorite) cocktails, from the French 75 ("I had my first of these in a dugout in the Argonne. I couldn't tell whether a shell or the drink hit me.") to the Louisville Pendennis Club's Old-Fashioned ("in honor of a famous old-fashioned Kentucky Colonel. I claim it was worthy of him").

Of his hometown, Cobb said, "Here in Paducah one encounters, I claim, an agreeable blend of Western kindliness, and Northern enterprises, superimposed on a Southern background. Here, I claim, more chickens are fried, more hot biscuits are eaten, more corn pone is consumed, and more genuine hospitality is offered than in any town of like size in the commonwealth." After his death in 1944, Cobb was buried in Oak Grove Cemetery in Paducah with an epitaph reading, "Back Home."

A ROAD TRIP TO FULTON COUNTY TO HONOR THE INVENTOR ★ OF THE STEAMBOAT ★

The importance of the Ohio and Mississippi Rivers can't be understated when it comes to the growth of the bourbon industry. Equally important though is the mode of transportation. Rivers only flow in one direction—unless the Mississippi is flowing backward, but that's a story in another book—and it's awfully difficult to ship something against the current without some extra power.

Enter the Industrial Revolution and Mr. Robert Fulton. Though another industrialist had been sailing steamboats on the Delaware River, his funding couldn't match Fulton's, and steamboats began cruising the rivers under Fulton's . . . ahem, steam.

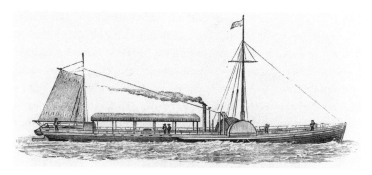

Robert Fulton's steamboat. Galloway, Robert Lindsay. *Fig. 49, — the "Clermont," 1807.* 1881. Photograph. Retrieved from the Library of Congress, www.loc.gov/item/2006691758/. (Accessed November 7, 2017.)

The first steamboat to make the round-trip from Pittsburgh to New Orleans and back was the *Enterprise* in 1915. Within another five years, almost seventy steamboats were sailing the shipping channels between Kentucky and the rest of the country.

Fulton County, the westernmost county in Kentucky, is named in honor of Robert Fulton, the man who brought steam power to the waterways and helped put counties like Fulton on the map. Its prime placement at the junction of the Ohio and Mississippi Rivers made Fulton County an ideal shipping hub.

★ IF YOU GO ▶ Fulton County

After you reach the end of your drive, you'll want to restore your strength with a snack, and the only appropriate snack to honor Fulton County is a banana. There are very few places in the United States that can grow bananas, and you're right, Kentucky isn't one of them. But what Kentucky lacks in climate, it makes up for in good infrastructure.

Bananas are grown in Central and South America, and the most important shipping hub for import from the United States' southern neighbors is New Orleans. The trip from New Orleans to warehouses in Chicago—from which the bananas were distributed across the country—couldn't be completed without a stop in between. Known at one time as the "Banana Capital of the World," Fulton County had the only icehouse between the port and the warehouses, where bananas shipped by the United Fruit Company could be re-iced on their journey north. Railcars in Fulton were loaded with giant blocks of ice on top of which the bananas made the rest of the journey, fresh and chilled, to be distributed across the country. According to the Fulton County Tourism Commission, at one point, 70 percent of all the bananas consumed in the United States passed through Fulton, Kentucky.

If a peelable yellow fruit isn't quite enough for you, plan your trip to Fulton in September for the International Banana Festival! Attend the Banana Ball, enter the Banana Bake-Off, and eat your share of the largest banana pudding in the world—there's literally a ton to share.

A ROAD TRIP TO HICKMAN, TO GO NUTS AND SAIL ★ THE MIGHTY MISSISSIPPI ★

Mark Twain once called Hickman, Kentucky, "a pretty town, perched on a handsome hill." The county seat of Fulton County is indeed a pretty town, whose hill overlooks the mighty Mississippi River, from which Twain glimpsed the Bluegrass State. The westernmost county seat in the state, Hickman is held together by nuts and boats.

First, the nuts. Hickman is proud of its pecan crop, a delicious export that is only grown in the farthest western reaches of the state. Pecan trees grow wild along the banks of the Mississippi and have been harvested in Hickman for decades. While tree shakers and mechanical nut crackers help make the work a bit easier in modern times, pecans were originally collected by hand from yards, farms, and the riverbanks to be sold across the country. And it's the other half of the equation—the boats—that help get them there. Its spot on the Mississippi River makes Hickman an ideal shipping point for one of Kentucky's rarest cash crops.

Hickman is known for its pecans and is ideally situated for travel between Kentucky and Missouri.

Hickman is also ideally situated for anyone looking to travel from Kentucky to Missouri. The Dorena-Hickman Riverboat Ferry is the last ferry crossing still operating between the only two border states that are not connected by road.

★ **IF YOU GO** **Hickman**

Autumn is the season to go west, not only for the weather and beauty of the changing season in the state but also for the Pecan Festival in downtown Hickman. The county seat celebrates its heritage with a weekend of live music, events, and most essentially, pecan pie.

You'll also want to bring a bit of cash with you to take the Dorena-Hickman Riverboat Ferry across the river. It'll only cost you $2 to ride as a pedestrian over to Missouri and back to Kentucky again and $14 one-way by car. For a truly memorable cruise, snag one of the earliest runs at 7:00 a.m. to catch the sunrise over the river. Or, make your way to the crossing at your own pace and hit the call button to let the captain know you're there.

This ferry travels across the mighty Mississippi River between Hickman, Kentucky, and Dorena, Missouri.

★ MARK TWAIN IN KENTUCKY ★

"Now and then," Mark Twain wrote in *Life on the Mississippi*, "we had a hope that if we lived and were good, God would permit us to be pirates." Twain did indeed become a kind of pirate on his beloved Mississippi River, sailing between St. Louis and New Orleans via steamboat.

Twain's kinship with the river probably grew from his up-bringing in Hannibal, Missouri, but his affinity for the Bluegrass State came from his mother, Jane Lampton, who grew up in Columbia, Kentucky, in Adair County. Jane was born to an old Kentucky family—her grandfather, frontiersman William Casey, is the namesake for Casey County. Perhaps she told young Samuel Langhorne Clemens stories of her girlhood in the Bluegrass State that captured his imagination.

However, the peaceful stories of idyllic Kentucky weren't those that made it into Twain's writings; it was a vicious western Kentucky feud that warranted an entry in Twain's narrative *Life on the Mississippi* and that sparked the inspiration for the Grangerford-Shepherdson feud in *Huckleberry Finn*.

The Darnell and Watson families feuded in the New Madrid Bend—aka Bubbleland—for more than sixty years. According to Twain, "in no part of the South has the vendetta flourished more briskly, or held out longer between warring families, than in this particular region." There is no historical record or narrative history that tells us *why* the feud began. A popular explanation says that it may have been some matter about a horse or a cow, but no one knows for sure. Whatever the reason, six decades passed before the Watsons wiped out the Darnells, effectively ending the feud.

★ HELPFUL LINKS ★

City of Paducah   **www.paducahky.gov**
McCracken County Public Library Local and Family History
    mclib.net/blogs/history
Paducah Main Street   **www.paducahmainstreet.org**
    /Default.htm
Paducah Wall to Wall   **www.paducahwalltowall.com**
Works by Irvin S. Cobb at Project Gutenberg
    www.gutenberg.org/ebooks/author/559
Fulton County, Kentucky   **fultoncounty.ky.gov/Pages**
    /index.aspx

City of Hickman   **hickman.cityof.org**

Dorena-Hickman Toll Ferry   **www.dorena-hickman**
  ferryboat.com

Fulton, Kentucky, Banana Festival
  www.thebananafestival.com

Kentucky Nut Corporation   **www.kykernelpecans.com**

Black's Pecan   **www.blackpecans.com**

Mark Twain, *Life on the Mississippi* at Project Gutenberg
  www.gutenberg.org/ebooks/245

William E. Ellis. *Irvin S. Cobb: The Rise and Fall of an American
  Humorist*. University Press of Kentucky, 2017. **https://www**
  .kentuckypress.com/live/title_detail.php?titleid=3659

Mark Twain. ca. 1907. May 20. Photograph. Retrieved from the Library of Congress, www.loc.gov/item/2004672770/. (Accessed November 7, 2017.)

"We make fine bourbon. At a profit if we can, at a loss if we must. But always fine bourbon."

—*Julian "Pappy" Van Winkle*

Part Three
PROHIBITION AND BEYOND

Kentucky is crazy proud of its bourbon heritage, so it must have been extra crazy on the day it voted to make the production, importation, transportation, and consumption of its beloved spirit illegal. It's OK; we all make mistakes sometimes. At the time, folks didn't really see it as a misstep. In 1920, Prohibition was instituted by the US government after its people spoke: their country was alcoholic, violent, immoral, and unhealthy. Prohibiting liquor—with the exception of communion wine, of course—would fix all that.

Now how does that old saying go? The road to hell is paved with good intentions? Or something like that. Obviously, Prohibition didn't go as planned. What started as an attempt to correct the immoralities of society ended in police and government corruption, heavy drinking, and home brews of toxic proportions. So, the law was repealed, and while it took the bourbon industry a few years to recover—just 34 of the 157 distilleries that were open at the start of Prohibition reopened at its close—the 1950s were a golden age of bourbon production in Kentucky.

Today, bourbon enjoys arguably its greatest rise since the '50s as the world is catching on to what we Kentuckians have known all along: there's simply nothing better than a fine glass of bourbon with friends.

Harris & Ewing, photographer. *Woman holding poster "Abolish Prohibition!"*
United States, 1931. Photograph. Retrieved from the Library of Congress,
www.loc.gov/item/hec2013006376/. (Accessed November 7, 2017.)

9 | **Prohibition in Kentucky**

It seems impossible for a state as proud to be the birthplace of bourbon as Kentucky is to play any role in prohibiting the consumption of alcohol. But in November 1919, Kentucky voters narrowly approved a constitutional amendment banning the sale and distribution of alcohol in the state. This was two months before the Volstead Act took effect—on January 17, 1920—making America (officially) dry. The Eighteenth Amendment to the US Constitution is better known in this country's history

Above: African American man carrying a case of Four Roses whiskey on his shoulder, possibly confiscated by the US Internal Revenue Bureau. [Between 1921 and 1932.] Photograph. Retrieved from the Library of Congress, www.loc.gov /item/2010646258/. (Accessed July 03, 2017.)

as Prohibition, and despite being cheered by many at the time, Kentucky didn't take to giving up its bourbon any better than the other states did.

So are you as shocked as we are that such an act could pass? Well, historians say we really shouldn't be. In 1919, anti-alcohol fervor ran strong. Activists cited family violence, alcoholism, and political corruption and called for a cure for sinful behavior. In Lexington, churches celebrated when Prohibition went into effect. Many believed Prohibition to be a victory, touting improved health (debatable, have you heard of bathtub gin?), lower crime rates, and improved morality if even for just a little while.

This nationwide constitutional ban on the production, importation, transportation, and sale of alcoholic beverages remained in place from 1920 to 1933, but the thirteen years weren't easy or sober ones.

Police raided and seized, but so did others. In Lexington, all of the whiskey from the James E. Pepper Distillery on Old Frankfort Pike was stolen by gun-wielding bandits. College students put themselves through school by bootlegging; patrolmen supplemented their income by illegally selling liquor they confiscated. Not exactly the country's most moral phase, right?

Prohibition was complicated because the laws weren't cut and dry. For example, religious uses of wine were allowed and private ownership and consumption of alcohol weren't made illegal under federal law. With states left to determine bans on possession, laws were left to be disregarded, tax revenues were lost, and criminal gangs took control of the liquor supply for many cities, unleashing widespread crime. Prohibition also unleashed unexperienced distillers who carelessly crafted their spirits from creosote, lead toxins, and sometimes even embalming fluid. Yum!

Prohibition cost the country a lot of jobs, something the bourbon industry in Kentucky felt deeply. Not only did the distilling industry suffer losses, but ancillary businesses such as cooperages, bottle manufacturers, taverns, and even farmers were affected. So as the 1932 presidential election approached with the country in the midst of the Great Depression, it was pretty easy to conclude that what started out as the "Noble Experiment" was really quite ignoble.

A ROAD TRIP TO COVINGTON, HOME OF ★ THE KING OF BOOTLEGGERS ★

It's safe to assume that as soon as something is made illegal, there are going to be a fair number of people who want it and even more who know how to get it. It has to be one of the basic laws of nature, right? Right.

Rum-running, smuggling, bootlegging—these are all terms for the illegal business of transporting alcoholic beverages when forbidden by law. In Prohibition Kentucky, perhaps the most famous bootlegger was George Remus, who is often somewhat fondly called the King of Bootleggers. In a drawn-out clash between Louisville's newspaper, the *Courier-Journal*, and the local government over an article exposing corrupt officials in northern Kentucky, it was alleged that the history of the state's bootlegging corruption began with Remus.

Remus started his career in Chicago as a lawyer and the owner of a pharmacy. When Prohibition started in 1920, he saw an opportunity to make money. One man's loss, another man's gain and all that. The administration of President Warren G. Harding made it easy to get permits to transfer alcohol to a pharmacy, and Remus just happened to own one of those. He moved to Cincinnati, Ohio, to be closer to a source of whiskey in Kentucky and started the Drobbatz Chemical Company, obtaining a permit to sell alcohol as a pharmaceutical company. Remus hijacked shipments of alcohol to his company and sold it on the black market for greater profits. Unfortunately, Drobbatz Chemical Company lost its license in 1921 after getting caught selling seven hundred cases of whiskey from the Old 76 Distillery in Newport, Kentucky.

But this minor setback couldn't keep the King of Bootleggers out of the game. He moved operations across the Ohio River to

Covington, Kentucky, and licensed the Kentucky Drug Company. Records show Remus also owned S. N. Weil & Company, which owned one-third of the Pogue Distillery in Maysville, and the Burks Spring Distillery in Loretto and amassed a fortune of more than $40 million. He bought up distilleries and pharmaceutical companies, using them to obtain permits to withdraw whiskey from the warehouses, only to have his men rob the transport trucks. Remus was arrested in 1921 but bribed a guard to help orchestrate the robbery of Burks Springs Distillery so his company could retain and sell the liquor.

He was sent to prison in 1925 and enjoyed his time behind bars like any multimillionaire would. Of course, it certainly didn't help his situation when his wife ran off with the prohibition agent who Remus had tasked her with obtaining a pardon from. Ouch. Adding insult to injury, she filed for divorce, sold off all of her husband's assets, and tried to have Remus deported to Germany while she was at it. While we're not condoning what happened next, it is hardly surprising. Remus was released in 1927, and on the day their divorce was to be finalized, he shot and killed his wife. He escaped a murder sentence with a successful insanity plea but was never able to get back into the bootlegging business.

The King of Bootleggers died in 1952 and is buried in Falmouth Cemetery in Pendleton County, Kentucky. Historians say Remus changed the way the whiskey industry did business during Prohibition. Because of his early successes, the government was forced to consolidate warehouses to better keep track of aging whiskey.

★ IF YOU GO ▶ Covington

The beginnings of the culture-rich northern Kentucky town of Covington can be found at the junction of Second and Garrard Streets in a park commemorating the legendary George Rogers Clark. The property was once the site of a 150-acre farm owned by Thomas Kennedy, the founder of Covington, who named the

The Roebling Murals at the Covington waterfront depict the history of the town from 800 BC to present day.

town after General Leonard Covington, a famous hero of the War of 1812.

While you're in town, check out its rich architectural history. Covington has the second highest number of properties listed on the National Register of Historic Places in Kentucky (read: some pretty cool and very beautiful old buildings that served as the foundations of the state). Start in the Licking Riverside Historic District. Located at the confluence of the Ohio and Licking Rivers, this neighborhood features amazing nineteenth-century architecture and scenic river and city views.

Don't miss the Roebling Murals at the waterfront. These eighteen panels are painted on the floodwall along the Ohio River and depict the history of Covington from 800 BC to present day. The murals were painted by Robert Dafford, an artist from Lafayette, Louisiana, who also painted the murals on Paducah's flood wall.

Perhaps our favorite Covington treasure is MainStrasse, a nineteenth-century German neighborhood village that features unique shops and galleries and a variety of amazing restaurants,

MainStrasse is a nineteenth-century German neighborhood village that features unique shops and galleries and a variety of restaurants.

beer and bourbon pubs, and options for live music. Throughout the year, the village hosts a variety of fun festivals, gallery hops, pub crawls, and holiday celebrations. Our favorites include Mardi Gras in February, Maifest in May, Goettafest in June, Oktoberfest in September, and the Northern Kentucky Wine Festival in October. Take us with you, please!

The Origins of Moonshine

Hollywood loves to depict Prohibition in the glamorous image of the Roaring Twenties: speakeasies, flappers, gangsters, and bootlegging. But Prohibition in Kentucky was a bit different than the version in the movies. Liquor became illegal overnight but not necessarily unavailable. Wine, beer, and our favorite bourbons were available but at a much higher price. When the taverns and saloons closed, soft drink stands and nightclubs kept bottles behind the counter.

But across Kentucky during Prohibition, moonshine was the primary source of liquor. In most areas of the modern world, *moonshine* is really just a slang term for illegal

Moonshine is still distilled in many parts of rural Kentucky. True moonshine is much different than the kind you see marketed on liquor store shelves.

high-proof distilled spirits (see verb: *moonshining*). But in Kentucky, moonshine is an actual liquor typically made with corn mash—a combination of corn, barley, and rye—and distilled at night in the rural hills of the state to avoid discovery.

Moonshine is an important piece of history in eastern Kentucky's Appalachian region. Known by many nicknames—white liquor, white lightning, mountain dew, hooch, homebrew, white whiskey, corn liquor—it likely entered the state in the late eighteenth century with Scots-Irish immigrants from Northern Ireland. These settlers made their whiskey without aging it, something that became a tradition in Appalachia and how moonshine is still enjoyed today.

Moonshine has historically been an important source of income for many folks in eastern Kentucky. Much of the state's corn liquor was distilled in the hollers of Appalachia, where illegal, often homemade, stills are a long-standing tradition. During Prohibition, moonshine production increased tenfold. Stills sprang up on farms across the Bluegrass State, and the liquor was even made on a small scale in washtubs or bathtubs in city homes or businesses.

It's no secret that police corruption ran rampant during Prohibition, and there was easy, untaxed money to be made. Not subject to government regulations, poorly made moonshine can cause serious illness and even death.

Today, moonshine is still made in hollers across the state. Don't let the labels on bottles at the liquor store fool you. If it's being sold over the counter, it's not real moonshine. But if you're drinking it out of a Mason jar, you're probably on the right track.

A ROAD TRIP TO THE
★ PEPPER DISTILLERY IN LEXINGTON ★

The Bluegrass region of central Kentucky was well known for distilling great bourbon throughout the nineteenth century. Lexington was home to three nationally known distilleries, all located on Manchester Street: James E. Pepper Distillery, Old Tarr Distillery, and Old Elk Distillery.

When Prohibition took effect, the warehouse at James E. Pepper Distillery held about 2,600 barrels of bourbon. In December 1920, more than a dozen bandits climbed out of Town Branch Creek, which runs alongside the historic Pepper barrel houses, and attacked guards at the building. Just as at similar heists across the state, the robbers got away with a hefty amount of aging bourbon and were never caught.

The Distillery District in Lexington is built on the site of the old Pepper Distillery. Today, visitors will find Ethereal Brewing, Barrel House Distilling, and a collection of bars and restaurants on this historic land.

Among the roughly 140 distilleries in and around Lexington, Pepper Distillery was the only bourbon operation in the city to survive Prohibition. Despite a few robberies, the distillery still had decent stores of whiskey in its bonded warehouses, and the product was bottled and sold as legal medicinal whiskey. After Prohibition, the operation was bought and rebuilt, but by the 1950s, the combination of overproduction and evolving consumer tastes put it out of business.

The historic label of James E. Pepper was an unfortunate one to lose. Like all great Kentucky bourbons, this one had a story. Pepper was from one of Kentucky whiskey's first families and became famous as a Thoroughbred horse breeder. He founded Meadowthorpe Stable and Meadowthorpe Stud (still open today on Leestown Pike), and his barns were some of the first to have electricity and telephones. And while telephones in barns may sound strange, any Kentuckian can tell you that you haven't seen a barn until you've seen a Thoroughbred barn. Trust us, these are modern luxurious mansions. Pepper combined his two interests—horses and whiskey—with the filly Pure Rye, who won the Kentucky Oaks in 1886. In 1891, the world-famous African American jockey Isaac Murphy rode Pepper's colt Mirage in the Kentucky Derby to a fifth-place finish.

But back to the bourbon. Colonel James E. Pepper was a larger-than-life bourbon industrialist, and his brand was produced from the American Revolution through 1958. After that, the label of the man for whom the old-fashioned is rumored to have been invented (by a bartender at the famed Pendennis Club in Louisville) was lost for fifty years, until 2008, when Washington, DC, businessman Amir Peay, owner of Georgetown Trading Company, purchased the James E. Pepper 1776 label and made plans to reopen the distillery on its original grounds on Manchester Street in Lexington.

The new distillery is housed in one of the buildings built after Prohibition in 1936 on the site of Pepper's original 1897 distillery. In addition to the distillery, the multimillion-dollar project includes a museum of Peay's collection of Pepper memorabilia.

★ IF YOU GO ▶ **James E. Pepper Distilling Company**
Opened in late 2017, the distillery stands on the historic property along Lexington's Town Branch Creek where Colonel Pepper's original warehouses were built. This is firmly situated among one of Lexington's most up-and-coming areas, aptly named the Distillery District. Located just west of the Lexington Center and Rupp Arena on Manchester Street, the Distillery District offers a collection of establishments that give visitors a unique experience in the city's industrial birthplace. Enjoy live music, unique architecture, great food, and libations while you're in town.

Our favorites include Crank & Boom Ice Cream Lounge (might we recommend the bourbon ball or the blueberry lime cheesecake?), The Break Room (a great place to grab a drink), and Ethereal Brewing Company (an up-and-coming craft brewery).

How To Get a Drink

In general terms, Prohibition means that things are prohibited—see, we were paying attention to our English teachers. But the laws—both federal and state—during the US Prohibition weren't all that black and white. Some states were stricter than others, and despite laws, alcohol was everywhere.

Citizens who wanted to have liquor in their homes or to serve it at a party most often got it from a middleman who was getting it from a bootlegger. These middlemen were in the most innocent of places: a candy store, a barber shop, a pool hall, a gas station, or any number of other small businesses. For a sordid few years, Mary Todd Lincoln's girlhood home on West Main Street in Lexington fronted as a candy and soft drink store, but its main business was selling liquor out of the back rooms.

Saloons reinvented themselves as restaurants and kept bars in basements or back rooms. These were the subjects of Hollywood's glamorous speakeasies. Only customers with the right password were admitted. Similarly, private clubs required membership for admittance.

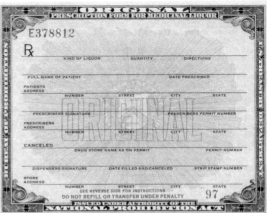

10 | **Medicinal Bourbon Permits**

While some visited the local candy store for their liquor, others relied on another popular workaround: their trusty doctor. Now, we've heard an old wives' tale or two about rubbing bourbon on the gums of teething babies (we introduce our Kentucky babies to bourbon early on), but a few teaspoons to nip asthma? That's not a remedy we're familiar with.

The Volstead Act allowed physicians to use government-issued forms to prescribe up to one hundred pints of whiskey every three months for certain illnesses. Licensed doctors advised their patients to take regular doses of hooch to cure ailments ranging from cancer and pneumonia to indigestion and depression. The Bureau of Prohibition audited the drugstores that filled these prescriptions—which were issued on preprinted government forms—but a few sheets from the prescription pad always disappeared one way or another.

In order for the doctors and pharmacists to write the prescriptions, someone had to be making the whiskey. Ten medicinal licenses were authorized, but just six distilleries applied for and received them: Brown-Forman, Glenmore (now part of Diageo, a British multinational alcoholic beverages company), Frankfort Distilling Company (now Four Roses Distillery), Schenley Distillery (now also a part of Diageo), American Medicinal Spirits (which became National Distillers and is now a part of Jim Beam), and A. Ph. Stitzel Distillery (the predecessor to Stitzel-Weller Distillery, also now a part of Diageo). Of these, Brown-Forman is the only company that still exists with its founding Brown family still at the company's helm.

These medicinal licenses permitted the distilleries to sell whiskey that was made before Prohibition went into effect, and after 1929, when that was running out, the licensed distilleries were allowed to produce three million gallons of spirits per year. A. Ph. Stitzel, which at the time was owned by Pappy Van Winkle, was the first distillery to begin producing spirits during Prohibition. Stitzel cooked up its first Prohibition batch in 1929, so its four-year-aged bourbon wasn't ready for consumption or sale before Prohibition ended in 1933. But at least Stitzel had a head start coming out of the dark ages.

Lucky bourbon collectors can still find one-pint bottles—the only way it was packaged—of Prohibition medicinal whiskey. Where whiskey produced before 1920 is extremely hard to get your hands on, that isn't the case with the whiskey bottled between 1920 and 1933. If you're a collector, a bottle of medicinal whiskey has a nice historical appeal, but that's about it. The product inside is known to be generally awful.

A ROAD TRIP TO THE
★ BROWN-FORMAN COOPERAGE ★

George Garvin Brown, a young pharmaceuticals salesman in Louisville saved and borrowed $5,500 and started J.T.S. Brown and Bro. with his half-brother in 1870. In the early days, they sold whiskey in sealed glass bottles, which was a bit odd in a time when the liquor was most commonly sold by the barrel. Old Forester Kentucky Straight Bourbon Whiskey was its first flagship brand, and the company went through several name and partnership changes before George Garvin Brown entered a partnership with George Forman, his accountant and friend, creating the now famous Brown-Forman. Don't you always wonder if partnerships like these knew they would grow to be one of the largest alcoholic beverage brands in the world a few centuries later?

Surviving centuries of changes in the bourbon industry and continuing operations even through the strict days of Prohibition, Brown-Forman now produces bourbon, whiskey, scotch, tequila, vodka, liqueur, and wine. We'll make no secret of our favorites—the Kentucky bourbon brands include Woodford Reserve, Old Forester, Early Times (not technically bourbon because it is aged in used barrels, but we'll include it anyway), and Cooper's Craft.

With an operation as large and dominant as Brown-Forman's, it is hardly a surprise that it manages its own cooperage. Brown-Forman Cooperage is where American white oak barrels are handcrafted for aging the brand's wide variety of liquors, and it is the only spirits company in the world to make its own barrels.

Touring the cooperage, guests have a chance to see the lumberyard, the selection of staves, and how the barrels are assembled—by hand—and charred. Personally, the barrel raising is our favorite part—watching each stave be hand selected to make the barrels airtight and smelling the burning oak. It's such an amazing craft.

A bourbon barrel being charred at the Kentucky Cooperage in Lebanon. To be bourbon, the whiskey must be stored in new charred oak barrels. Photo courtesy of the Independent Stave Company.

Equally as amazing is that what feels like a step back in time is actually an operating cooperage producing more than 1,500 barrels each day.

★ IF YOU GO   ### Kentucky's Cooperages

Tours of the Brown-Forman Cooperage in Louisville must be scheduled ahead of time through Mint Julep Tours at **mint juleptours.com**. If you can't make it to Jefferson County, visit the Kentucky Cooperage in Lebanon. Operated by the Independent Stave Company, tours are offered Monday through Friday. Closed-toe shoes are required, and children under sixteen years of age require adult supervision. Learn more at **www .iscbarrels.com/tours/**.

A ROAD TRIP TO
★ WOODFORD RESERVE DISTILLERY ★

There's always something about each Kentucky distillery tour that makes it as special as the brand itself. We've toured nearly all of the bourbon factories across the state, and we leave each one with a standout memory. At Maker's Mark, they let you dip your fingers in the sour mash (don't worry, the cooties cook out). Views don't get much better than the ones at Buffalo Trace. The architecture at Four Roses is something to be admired and remembered. And at Woodford Reserve in Versailles, there's just something about the barrels.

A long stone staircase stretches from the visitor's center down to the barrel houses. On our visit, we were sitting on these stairs enjoying a sandwich from the amazing Glenn's Creek Cafe on-site when distillery employees began rolling barrels across the road between rackhouses. By hand, they pushed, hand-over-hand, hand-over-hand, as they carefully moved barrel after barrel. Perhaps it was the scenic canopy of trees, it could have even been the delicious sandwich, but something made watching the back-breaking, hands-on work that goes into the craft of making bourbon incredibly memorable.

Woodford Reserve produces small-batch Kentucky Straight Bourbon Whiskey in four varieties: bourbon, double-oaked, rye whiskey, and the Master Distiller's annual collection. Distilling on this site began in 1780—as the Old Oscar Pepper Distillery and later as the Labrot & Graham Distillery—but the "modern" buildings were constructed in 1838. The buildings are listed on the National Register of Historic Places, and the distillery was designated in 2000 as a National Historic Landmark.

Woodford Reserve is one of the state's oldest and smallest distilleries and is where Elijah Pepper first began crafting his whiskey. On these same grounds, Master Distiller James Christopher Crow perfected his whiskey-making methods, which today have become common practice, including the implementation of sour

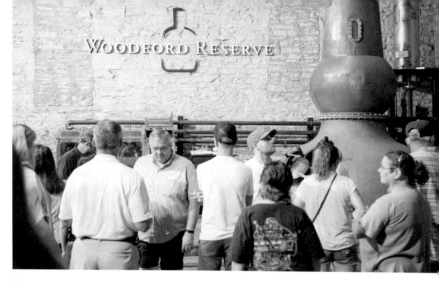

Visitors enjoy a tour of Woodford Reserve Distillery in Versailles.

mash into fermentation. The distillery includes a five-hundred-foot-long gravity-fed barrel run (where, like us, you can watch the barrels be moved around the property!) and one-hundred-year-old cypress wood fermenters. Visitors can also tour the only heat-cycled barrel houses in the world, which are designed to ensure more liquor seeps into the charred white oak, giving Woodford Reserve bourbon its color and signature flavor.

★ IF YOU GO ▶ Woodford Reserve Distillery

This picturesque distillery sits about eight miles outside of Versailles off US 60 between Interstate 64 and Versailles. The drive there is almost as beautiful as the tour through the grounds. Not far from the birthplace of bourbon along the banks of the Kentucky River, Woodford Reserve is truly in the heart of bourbon country. Visitors can take a guided educational tour through the distillery that explains the history of bourbon, its unique five sources of flavor, the bottling process, and more. Sample the product at the visitor center and stay for lunch at the delicious Glenn's Creek Cafe! Learn more at **www.woodford reserve.com**. Woodford is a stop on the Kentucky Bourbon Trail, so don't forget your passport!

Concentration Warehouses

In the early days of Prohibition, the warehouses at distilleries across the state held hundreds of barrels of aging bourbon. Just because it was illegal to make didn't mean it all got tossed in the river. Kentuckians aren't wasteful. With a lack of security, particularly at the more rural distilleries, this aging whiskey became the target of burglars and gangsters. Several warehouses were robbed and burned; others were drained of their bourbon and the barrels filled with water. After a couple of years, the government decided they probably should take care of this problem.

The Liquor Concentration Act of 1922 required that all bourbon whiskey stored in bonded warehouses be concentrated into newly designated warehouses that were heavily guarded to protect the remaining liquor inventory. In Kentucky, these warehouses were located in Lexington, Bardstown, Frankfort, and Louisville.

11 | The Impact of Kentucky Bourbon on World War II

While many advocated for Prohibition at its beginning, there truly is no keeping Kentuckians from their bourbon. Why, whatever would we put in our julep cups? In the last year of Prohibition, around 80 percent of the Bluegrass State was calling for its repeal. On December 5, 1933, Congress ratified the Twenty-First Amendment, officially repealing Prohibition. Kentucky was one of the three-fourths of the country's states that voted for

Above: Industrial Alcohol Production for the War Department. ca. 1942.
Photograph. Retrieved from the Library of Congress, www.loc.gov/pictures
/resource/fsa.8e11010/. (Accessed November 7, 2017.)

repeal, but the ban on alcoholic beverages didn't lift in Kentucky immediately. The state's constitutional amendment repealing Prohibition wasn't ratified until November 1935.

After fifteen years of closure, many operations didn't survive, but by 1937, there were seventy-seven distilleries operating in Kentucky. However, what's a storied history without a long, rocky road to haul? The distilling industry had really no more than just started gearing back up when the United States entered World War II, and the federal government once again halted alcoholic beverage production. This time, it wasn't for moral reasons. We had apparently learned (or maybe not learned) our lesson there. Instead, the government instructed distilleries to switch to producing grain-neutral, 190 proof industrial alcohol to be used in ammunition, fuel, antifreeze, plastics, and other needed materials during wartime.

The repurposed distilleries were also tasked with making the recently invented penicillin antibiotic. Penicillin—which was discovered in 1928 by Scottish scientist Alexander Fleming—is a product of fermentation, so distilleries had a leg up in production knowledge and facilities when mass quantities of the antibiotic were needed.

Distilleries produced 1.7 billion gallons of industrial alcohol during World War II. In 1945, the industry returned to bourbon distilling. At the start of the Korean War just five years later, distillers across the state held their breath and increased production dramatically, anticipating wartime restrictions. This time, no orders came, and everyone was left with excessive inventory. This doesn't really sound like the worst thing to happen, right? But government bond restrictions on production and inventory made it difficult to sell what was made. To help deplete the distillers' excess inventories, the federal government extended bonding periods. And everyone just drank a little bit faster.

After the wars, Americans once again had money to spend, and the distilleries were prepared with product for them to spend it on.

The site of the former Seagram's Distillery on South Seventh Street in Louisville is part of a large complex of unique architecture that today is used by several corporations. Seagram's discontinued its bourbon production during World War II to produce industrial alcohol.

A ROAD TRIP TO THE
OLD SEAGRAM'S DISTILLERY AND
★ MICHTER'S DISTILLING COMPANY ★

Following the end of Prohibition, Seagram's Distillery opened on South Seventh Street in Louisville. It joined a collection of distilleries all together in present-day Shively and officially opened for operation in 1937. A crowd of seventy-one thousand people attended the opening in Louisville during the week of the Kentucky Derby (there's that magic Kentucky duo again, horses and bourbon), and at the time, Seagram's claimed to be the largest distillery in the world.

Like other distilleries, during World War II, Seagram's stopped making its Seagram's Seven Crown and Kessler Whiskey to produce industrial alcohol.

The complex of buildings is unique. Designed by the Louisville architecture firm Joseph & Joseph, the main office building was built in the Regency revival style, and the art deco brick warehouses included a system of underground tunnels so barrels of bourbon could be moved around the complex without being seen by the public.

Much to our dismay—who doesn't want a tour of those tunnels?!—Seagram's closed in 1983, and the old distillery complex is now divided up into several operations, including a vegetable oil and shortening company, Golden Foods / Golden Brands. However, just around the corner (literally on the same block but located on cross street Wathen Lane), visitors can find Michter's Distillery, a craft distillery that makes high-end bourbon.

Michter's Distilling Company produces three whiskeys—American Whiskey, Kentucky Straight Rye Whiskey, and Sour Mash Whiskey—and one bourbon, with only the bourbon containing more than 51 percent corn and the rye whiskey made up predominantly of rye. It claims to be part of the founding of the first American whiskey company in 1753, and we're not going to dispute that. We have a hard enough time keeping the bourbon distillers in their corners; we're not refereeing the whiskey historians, too.

Michter's reinvented itself in the 1990s, honoring its rich history but shifting focus to the product it was crafting. Through little details like toasting the barrels before they are charred to ensure the wood's sugars are more accessible, Michter's works to create fine whiskeys. In 2016, Michter's Distillery announced it would double its production capacity of five hundred thousand proof gallons per year to one million proof gallons by adding a second shift and four new fermenters.

Facing: Michter's bourbon is now distilled less than a block from the old Seagram's Distillery on South Seventh Street, but visitors can tour its location in downtown Louisville on Whiskey Row.

Tours are not available at the distilling location in Shively near the old Seagram's Distillery. But the architecture firm that designed the original Seagram's complex and the Michter's Distillery building is restoring a four-story historic building in Louisville's Main Street District, which will be home to Michter's urban bourbon distillery. Extensive structural modifications will allow for a fully functioning distillery with two replica eighteenth-century pot stills, a fermenting tank, barrel filling, a barrel storage area, a bottling line, and a tour mezzanine through the distillery to end in a gift shop and tasting area. When complete, the tour experience will wind through the distillery educating visitors about each stop from grain handling through barrel storage and bottling. Learn more at **www.michters.com**.

World War II Memorials Across Kentucky

Honor those Kentuckians who fought for our country at some absolutely beautiful memorials across the state. Here are a few favorites from our travels:

The Bataan War Memorial in Harrodsburg

Cave Hill Cemetery in Louisville

The Mayfield WWII Monument in Mayfield

The Illinois Central Railroad WWII Monument in Paducah

The WWII Memorial in Paducah City Hall

The Hopkins County Courthouse WWII Memorial in Madisonville

The Jefferson County WWII Memorial in Louisville

The Campbell County WWII Monument in Newport

12 | The Distillers' Association and the Modern Bourbon Industry

In May of 1964, Congress declared bourbon whiskey to be a "distinctive product" to the United States, which gave bourbon geographical protection. This declaration meant that no other country could label its liquors as "bourbon" and sealed the marketing ability of manufacturers of bourbon to sell it as "America's spirit." Now, what's more patriotic than that?

Above: Glasses lined up at the tasting bar at Four Roses Distillery in Anderson County. Visitors can tour the distillery and sample the product at this location before traveling to Bardstown to the bottling facility for another tasting.

At that time—and it remains true today—Kentucky was producing the lion's share of America's bourbon. By 1968, there were almost nine million barrels of bourbon aging in warehouses across the Bluegrass State. Considering there are just under five million people living in Kentucky, we are outnumbered by our bourbon barrels. What a wonderful problem to have!

Today, bourbon production shows incredible volume and sales gains. As the rest of the world catches on to what Kentuckians have enjoyed for years, the state's distillers lay down nearly two million barrels annually. Export volume growth is increasing as well, something the Kentucky Distillers' Association credits to product innovation, improved access, and consumer premium-ization. Basically, the bourbon drinkers are paying more attention to what's in their glass and the bourbon industry is responding with better bourbons than ever.

Each year on June 14, we celebrate Kentucky's (well, OK, America's) native spirit with National Bourbon Day. By now, we're all familiar with the government's list of rules as to what qualifies a whiskey to have the proud title of "bourbon," but some folks take it a bit further and contend that if it ain't made in Kentucky, it ain't bourbon. Who are we to argue? Bourbon is arguably the state's signature industry, and 95 percent of the world's bourbon is made right here in the Bluegrass State.

We owe a toast to Elijah Craig, who helped establish the state of Kentucky and who started one of the first distilling operations in Georgetown. We owe a toast to Colonel Edmund H. Taylor Jr., who built the majestic Old Taylor Distillery on the banks of the Kentucky River and fathered the modern bourbon tourism industry. We'll pour a glass for Catherine Carpenter, Marjorie Samuels, Mary Jane Blair, Marianne Barnes, and all of the other women who helped the industry grow to what it is today. And to the Beams, the Peppers, the Wellers, the Van Winkles, the Browns, and all of the other founding families of Kentucky Straight Bourbon Whiskey, we'll drink to your ingenuity, your dedication, your perseverance, and your good taste.

The Kentucky Distillers' Association

Thirty-two distillers met at the Galt House Hotel in Louisville in 1880 and organized in order to protect bourbon from "needless and obstructive laws and regulations." The group fought for decades to reduce whiskey taxes, shrink insurance fees, and address other issues as they arose. The organization disbanded during Prohibition and was reorganized in 1936. In the decades that followed, the Kentucky Distillers' Association has served as a strong advocate on distilled spirits issues, including state- and federal-level battles over taxes.

In 1999, the association created the Kentucky Bourbon Trail, which rocketed bourbon tourism into one of the state's fastest growing attractions. More than 2.5 million people from all 50 states and more than 50 countries have visited distilleries on the tour.

So while the bourbon industry has changed and evolved over the course of 130 years, the basic mission of the Kentucky Distillers' Association remains the same: to protect the trade interests of the industry whenever they may be threatened and to handle common problems in a concerted action.

Your legacy lives on in every Kentuckian and every bourbon connoisseur.

A ROAD TRIP TO THE ★ KENTUCKY BOURBON FESTIVAL ★

What's the one thing better than celebrating Kentucky bourbon? Celebrating bourbon among tens of thousands of fellow Kentuckians and bourbon enthusiasts. This huge annual festival mixes black-tie events with golf outings, hot rod runs, and family fun. Oh, and there is a lot of bourbon to drink there, too.

Festival goers enjoy tastes of their favorite bourbons at elaborately constructed distillery models at the Kentucky Bourbon Festival in Bardstown. The festival is held every September.

In September each year, Bardstown's thirteen thousand residents more than triple for a week. Rain or shine—we've been there for both, and we suggest boots in the rain—the Kentucky Bourbon Festival is a six-day event of smooth bourbon, delicious food, great entertainment, and a healthy dose of Kentucky hospitality. It's our absolute favorite.

★ IF YOU GO ▸ The Kentucky Bourbon Festival
Head to One Court Square in Bardstown around the middle of September each year, and prepare your palates. Each brand has a tent, and each tent has a taste. There are also events for kids and families with arts and crafts, live music, food, shows, and plenty of Kentucky culture. The festival is free, but some events charge admission. Visit **www.kybourbonfestival.com** to learn more.

Does Prohibition Still Haunt Kentucky?

These days, most consider Prohibition to be something of the past. It's those dark days we don't like to talk about. But in Kentucky, one has to wonder: is it really over? In many of our counties, the sale of alcohol is still a hot-button issue, and when an alcohol vote is on the ballot (which is nearly every election), it can be a major hullabaloo.

While most of the population of the state is concentrated in wet counties—meaning counties in which alcohol can be bought and served—Kentucky has more dry counties than wet ones. And the wet-dry classification isn't all that cut and dried. There are limitations like "moist" and "limited-50" and "small farm winery." It's tough to keep up, right?

At the heart of the debate are the same beliefs that plagued the country in the years leading up to Prohibition: that alcohol is evil or immoral or unhealthy. Like Prohibition, it is tough to say which side is right and which is wrong. What is clear? We're going to have differing opinions for years to come.

★ HELPFUL LINKS ★

Aaron D. Purcell, "Bourbon to Bullets: Louisville's Distilling Industry during World War II, 1941–45," *Register of the Kentucky Historical Society* 96, no. 1 (Winter 1998): 61–87: **http://www.jstor.org/stable/23383666**

The Filson Historical Society **filsonhistorical.org/the-king -of-the-bootleggers-and-kentucky/**

The Frazier History Museum: **fraziermuseum.org /prohibition-and-kentucky/**

The Lexington Distillery District **www.lexingtondistillery district.com**

James E. Pepper Distilling Company **jamesepepper.com**

L.A. Whiskey Society   **www.lawhiskeysociety.com**
Brown-Forman   **www.brown-forman.com**
Craft Distillery Tours   **craftdistillerytours.com**
Joseph & Joseph Architects   **josephandjoseph.net**
Michter's Distilling Company   **www.michters.com**
Kentucky Distillers' Association **kybourbon.com**
Kentucky Bourbon Festival   **www.kybourbonfestival.com**

Glossary of Bourbon Terms

angel's share The portion of bourbon in an aging barrel that is lost to evaporation.

barrel proof Whiskey bottled at the desired proof while aging in a barrel. No water is added before bottling, so these bourbons are higher proof than others.

bung The stopper used to seal a barrel.

charring The process that sets fire to the interior of barrels for less than one minute and creates a layer of charred wood.

continuous still A giant apparatus in which the main component is a very tall metal column used to separate the alcohol from the water in the distiller's beer by vaporizing the alcohol content.

cooperage The making of barrels and casks. In the bourbon industry, the location where the charred white oak barrels are crafted.

distiller's beer The thick, fermented mash of cooked grains, water, and yeast that is transferred from the fermenter to the beer still for the first distillation.

fermentation The process by which yeast transforms sugar into alcohol and carbon dioxide.

fermenter A giant tub made of metal or cypress where the mash of cooked grains and water meet the yeast. The yeast begins to act on sugars in the grain, and fermentation occurs over a few days.

mash The mixture of cooked grains and water before the yeast is added to start fermentation.

mashbill The grain recipe used to make bourbon.

mash tub A large tub where grains are combined with water and cooked to soften them and break down the starch into simple sugars before the resulting mash is transferred to the fermenter.

proof The measurement of beverage alcohol on a scale of 200 (in America). A 100 proof spirit contains 50 percent alcohol.

rackhouse The building where whiskey is aged, sometimes referred to as the warehouse or the rickhouse.

ricks The wooden structures on which barrels of bourbon rest during aging.

single-barrel bourbon Bourbon drawn from one barrel that has not been mingled with any other bourbons.

small-batch bourbon A product of mingling select barrels of bourbons that have matured into a specific style.

Cameron M. Ludwick is a bookworm, trivia nerd, and former band geek who still relies on the survival skills she learned at Girl Scout camp to cope with nature. A Kentucky native, she now has bigger hair and lives in Austin, Texas.

Blair Thomas Hess is a born-and-bred Kentuckian who once won a sack-the-pig contest at the Trigg County Country Ham Festival. She resides in Frankfort with her daughter and her picture-taking, bourbon-collecting husband.

Together, these longtime friends travel across the Commonwealth of Kentucky, exploring its various wonders and uncovering its best-kept secrets. They are the authors of *My Old Kentucky Road Trip.*

Follow the adventure at **www.myoldkentuckyroadtrip.com.**
Twitter: **@MyOldKYRoadTrip**
Instagram: **@myoldkentuckyroadtrip**